Contents

Introduction: So You Want to Be a Sales Professional

If you are reading this book, there is a good chance that you are either new to sales or looking to recharge your sales career. In the latter circumstance, you may have forgotten more about sales than most people remember. No matter what the circumstance, you have purchased the right book.

If you are new to sales, you are about to enter one of the most exciting professions in the world. Sales is not a fallback career that you enter because nothing else appeals to you. Sales can be one of the most intellectually stimulating and financially rewarding careers in the world. Very few people earn more than the best sales professionals in their respective fields. Also, very few people have the opportunity to create something from nothing every day. When you apply your product or service to the customer's business in exactly the right way, you have created something special—the solution to a business problem and the possibility of helping your customer be successful.

This is what I mean when I say that sales is an incredibly rewarding profession. That is, in sales, you have the opportunity to create something from nothing, which is a rewarding way to earn a living.

Sales gives you the opportunity to use all of your brain power to create great solutions for your customers. Every selling situation is different in some way. That is, many customer needs are similar, allowing you to leverage your prior success, but no two selling situations are *exactly* the same. This gives you the unique opportunity to go where no sales person has gone before.

If you are not new to sales, but a field-tested veteran, you may have forgotten why you got into sales in the first place. For you, sales may have become a hard way to earn a living. You may have reached a point in your career at which making that next sale is laborious. But you have purchased this book to get you back on track. At this stage, you cannot afford to start over in a new career. Rather, you must renew the fire in your belly that was there when you started in the business.

This book is written by a sales professional who cherishes the opportunity to be called a sales *professional*. And I place emphasis on the word *professional* because sales is no less of a profession than is that of doctor, lawyer, or accountant. My goal in this book is to provide a complete system for sales success. This system is based on my three-step sales process: Plan, Execute, and Close—PEC, for short.

Consistent with this sales process, the book is divided into three parts. Part I is called "World-Class Sales Planning," and it is in this part that I discuss the "triple crown" of sales planning: prospecting planning, territory planning, and account planning. I do not provide a comprehensive process for any of these three areas of sales planning. Rather, because I am helping you lay a strong foundation for selling success throughout your career, I select one or two high-impact ideas from each area that you can implement immediately. Prospecting planning is covered in Chapter 1, designed to help you get your sales career off to a quick start. If you are a field-tested veteran, on the other hand, expect an almost immediate increase in sales opportunities once you implement those Chapter 1 ideas. Chapter 2 is devoted to the crown jewel of sales planning: territory planning. As you will see, your territory plan is, in effect, your sales business plan; both the prospecting plan and the accounts plan support your overall territory development strategy, as documented in the territory plan. Thus, Chapter 2 also introduces my large-account strategy. If implemented, this strategy will vault you to the top of your industry in terms of selling success. Chapter 3 completes the discussion of sales planning and focuses on account planning. As you will learn, sound account planning led a sales professional in my first company to what we considered to be the "greatest sale in the world" at that time. If you implement what I tell you in Chapter 3, you too can generate your own "world's greatest sale."

The next logical step after sales planning is sales execution. Part II explains my sales process, or Execute, and is titled "High-Performance Sales Execution." It also has three chapters.

When you first get started in sales, you have no customers and no associated revenue, so the need for prospecting is quite apparent. However, as you become more successful, the need for prospecting seems less clear and soon you may not prospect at all. But, because you have not been keeping your sales pipeline filled with new opportunities, you are left with few, if any, sales opportunities—you are in a "sales valley." When this happens, you prospect again, and if you stick with it long enough, you resume your former level of success (peak), only to repeat the process throughout your career. Fortunately, these sales peaks and valleys have an easy-to-implement solution, which I show you in Chapter 4.

When you successfully complete a prospecting call, you get to the most important phase of the process: sales discovery. This is the point at which you work with the customer either face-to-face (if you are a field seller) or over the telephone (if you are a

tele-seller) to ask a series of open-ended questions that will reveal customer needs. It is only through the sales discovery process that you can create those winning solutions, as well as
differentiate your solutions in a competitive market. The sales-
discovery process is discussed in Chapter 5.

Invariably, over the course of a given sales cycle, the customer will ask for clarification, and this clarification process is
often called a "sales objection." That is, the customer may tell
you that your price is too high, or he may believe that he already
has a similar solution from the competition. If the customer
mentions the competition during the process, it usually comes
early and often—this is called the "competition objection."
Chapter 6 shows how to manage the objection by welcoming its
arrival in the sales process!

To enjoy the fruits of the sales process, Part III takes you to
the third step: the close.

There are many ways to close a sale. For instance, you can
first review the solution you have proposed and then ask a question such as, "Are you ready to proceed with the order?" This is
a technique called the "direct close," but it is effective. In Chapter 7, I review the different types of closing techniques and show
how to incorporate them into the sales process.

For some sales, typically larger sales, you may also be asked
to deliver a presentation to a purchasing committee or to write a
proposal. Sales presentations and proposals are crucial tools in
the sales process, so in Chapters 8 and 9, respectively, I show
how they can greatly improve your success rate.

Chapter 10 provides ten strategies that you can take along on
your journey to sales excellence.

PART I

World-Class Sales Planning

CHAPTER I

Prospecting Plans
Keeping the Pipeline Full

Most sales professionals do not like to plan. Their classic argument is that planning time takes away from selling time in the field. They could sell more if they didn't have to waste time drawing up plans to sell.

If you are new to sales, you have a unique opportunity to start your career off on the right foot. That is, you can develop good sales habits as opposed to bad ones. The decision to forgo planning is a poor choice you could make as a new sales professional, and it would establish one of those bad habits. Instead, right from the beginning you can make planning a regular part of your sales procedures. On the other hand, if you are a seasoned sales person looking to reinvigorate your sales career, then planning is a great place for you to start the process.

Planning Is a Natural Part of Living

If you think about it, we plan our daily lives in a variety of ways:

❏ You plan a course of study when you begin college so that you can graduate with expertise in your chosen field.

❑ You plan when you decide to go on a vacation.

❑ You plan for your financial future and retirement.

If we look at planning from the opposite perspective—that is, the idea of *not planning*—the results lead us to the same conclusion:

❑ How many games would a team win if its coach didn't have a game plan?

❑ Would you invest in a fledgling company whose entrepreneur didn't show you a business plan?

❑ How nice will your life be if you haven't saved enough money for your retirement?

If you consider these examples, it is quite clear that planning is an integral part of daily life, and it must be part of the sales process as well. For instance, what degree of success could you possibly have if you approached a major account without a sales plan or account plan? We are all familiar with the phrase "Work smart, not hard." That's what planning is all about—working smart and making every effort count.

Yet, for some reason, sales planning has gotten a bad reputation. My guess is that the bum rap is a result of all the day-to-day pressures that are part of a sales career. Sales people have goals that have to be met, whether weekly, monthly, quarterly, or annually, depending on management and the industry. It's difficult to live under a microscope like that. And the measurements and metrics do not stop with periodic sales goals. There are pipeline metrics, gross margin metrics, and phone metrics (if you work in a telesales organization or a call center). Facing a never-ending stream of measurements and management scrutiny, sales people say it's hard to think about doing anything other than meeting those goals. So, the general lack of interest in sales planning (and that's putting it nicely) is more a matter of situation than of philosophy. The idea of planning seems great; the problem is being able to devote the time and energy it takes to reap the rewards of any planning efforts. No matter how difficult it is to find the time to plan, *not planning* does much more of a disservice to you as a sales professional. Planning is an integral part of life and an integral part of sales. In telling yourself (or your manager) that you do not have the time to plan, you are only making excuses for yourself that ultimately will limit your ability to be successful, in both the short and long term.

The important thing to remember is that sales professionals work in a resource-constrained environment, and time is one of those resources. You could say that you don't have time to plan, but any good time-management book will tell you otherwise.

In sales, planning is the only proper response to this dilemma. In fact, in my book *Red Hot Cold Call Selling* (AMACOM, 2006), I make the point that the business of sales is "selling as much as you can, given the time permitted." This can be done only with good sales planning, no matter what anyone else says. You must *plan* in order to be successful.

You Are the CEO of Your Own Territory

Perhaps the best way to think about sales planning is to view a company CEO from a sales perspective. That is, the major difference between a CEO and a sales professional is the size of each person's territory. The CEO's territory is either the entire world or the smaller region that the company does business in. That

CEO's sales territory is then divided up and given to the sales people in the company.

The sales person's territory is simply a subset of the CEO's territory. The CEO is responsible for making sure the company reaches its sales objectives. Likewise, the sales professional is responsible for making sure that he or she achieves the objectives for that individual territory. Because the only substantive difference between the sales territory and the CEO's territory is size, successful accomplishment of the objectives requires the same types of activities.

Now, what would you think of a CEO who did not have a business plan? Not much, probably. The same can be said of the sales professional. Remember, you are the CEO of your own territory, and so it is crucial that you develop a plan to achieve maximum success, given the time and resources at your disposal, as well as the nature of the accounts in your territory.

Sales Planning Essentials

I have limited the discussion of planning to the most crucial elements for getting started. That is, I share with you three essential tools for sales planning.

1. A prospecting business plan

2. A territory plan

3. An account plan

These tools are interrelated, and together they provide your overall sales business plan. The remainder of this chapter discusses the first tool, the prospecting business plan.

Your Prospecting Business Plan

Designed to help you grasp the effort involved in being success-ful in sales, the *prospecting business plan* helps you avoid the sell-ing peaks and valleys referred to in the Introduction.

If salespeople were able to maintain a consistent time invest-ment in the prospecting process, the selling peaks and valleys would be rare occurrences. The fact that these selling peaks and valleys are prevalent demonstrates how great the need is to ad-dress this matter in the first chapter of this book.

Sales peaks and valleys—especially the valleys—are costly. To understand just how costly they can be, let's take a look at three broad categories of activities that sales professionals typi-cally engage in.

1. *Opportunity management.* Some of a sales professional's activities involve existing opportunities. These activities start when the opportunity is first identified and continue through the sales process, up to and including the close of the sale.

Examples of opportunity-management activities are attend-ing a face-to-face meeting after the opportunity has been identi-fied, writing sales proposals, preparing and delivering sales presentations, writing letters and e-mails, and making telephone calls.

Opportunity management even includes administrative ac-tivities, such as following through on purchase orders, helping the accounting department complete a credit check, or assisting the accounting department in preparing invoices in formats specified by the customers.

2. *Prospecting.* When you thing about prospecting, consider all of the activities that sales people engage in to identify new opportunities. These include cold calling, letter writing, and

e-mails; research on the Internet (say, to learn about a company); and preparing or updating account plans as they relate to new opportunities.

When you think of prospecting activities, think as broad and comprehensive as possible—as comprehensive as opportunity management. For instance, it includes holding a seminar attended by a room of prospects, as would the preparation and delivery of a speech at your annual industry conference if the conference were attended by companies in your target market.

3. *Nonselling activities.* In stark contrast to the two other categories, nonselling activities are residuals—everything not included in the first two categories. Typically, there are only a few activities in this category, such as training, sales meetings, and completing expense reports. It is important to note that most of the activities you might be tempted to place in this category really belong in the other two groups.

For instance, you might think that planning is a nonselling activity. However, planning clearly belongs in one of the other two categories, depending on whether the planning is for existing opportunities or to identify new opportunities.

Another activity traditionally placed in this category is the paperwork associated with completing a sales transaction, such as purchase orders, contracts, and other required documentation. However, paperwork is an opportunity-management activity, since it pertains to existing sales opportunities.

Why I am telling you all of this? Because we need to be clear on the definitions of these terms, mentioned throughout this book. The reason there are selling peaks and valleys is that sales people tend to overinvest in opportunity management and underinvest in prospecting. The explanation for this situation is the generalized "fear of rejection."

Most sales professionals would prefer to do anything, including knowingly having a sales strategy that produces less income, than address their fears of rejection and consequently earn higher income. Because we try to avoid rejection, we spend more time with known prospects, as we can anticipate fewer rejections than from new opportunities. As a result, we implement a less-than-optimal sales strategy. You will sell more and earn more if you make the appropriate investments in both categories of sales activities.

Apportion Your Time

By managing your time well, as you will learn in this book, you can make those investments in both categories and optimize your sales and income as a result. This will become clearer when you refer to Figure 1.1, which illustrates the apportionment of time for sales planning activities.

The first thing that you should notice about Figure 1.1 is that there are three categories of sales professionals: new, moderate,

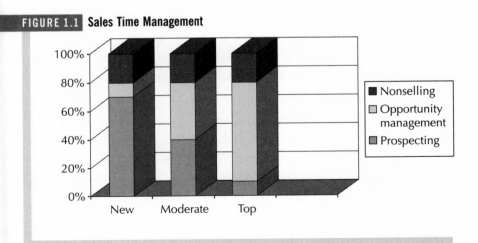

FIGURE 1.1 Sales Time Management

and top. A seller in the "new" category is not generating much in the way of current opportunities. These sellers are the lower performers on the sales team (at the moment), owing to their relatively low number of opportunities in the sales pipeline. A "moderate" seller has a moderate level of opportunities in the sales pipeline. Last are the sellers with many current sales opportunities. These are the top sellers in an organization, and they have noticeably more current opportunities in their sales pipeline.

Note in Figure 1.1 how the magnitude of nonselling activities does not vary much in relation to the opportunity category for each sales type. After all, if sales training and sales meetings are two key elements in the nonselling category, all sellers on the team must sit through the seminar to complete the program. Likewise, all sellers sit through the sales meeting. The point is that there are no economies of scale for sales training or team meetings as they relate to the different categories of sales professionals. Thus, we can expect the time allocated for these activities is relatively fixed.

Another interesting point about nonselling activities is that typically they are not at the discretion of the sales person. When the manager calls a sales meeting or decides to hold a training session for the team, everyone is required to attend. The sales person does not get to decide how much time he or she chooses to allocate to nonselling activities. Thus, the matter of time management in the area of sales is best summarized by answering this question: How does one allocate selling time between prospecting activities and opportunity-management activities?

Most sellers would prefer to be closing a deal or working an active opportunity rather than prospecting for new opportunities. Yet overinvesting in opportunity management works to the detriment of prospecting for new sales opportunities. How do you balance the two? By making a fixed and measurable daily commitment to performing the prospecting activities. This is exactly what the prospecting business plan is designed to do.

The Model for the Plan and Its Variant

The prospecting business plan is presented in Figure 1.2. While the figure is not terribly sophisticated, it is an important report. The first line of the plan is the current year's sales goal. (Experienced sales people will be quite familiar with that figure.) Figure 1.3 is a plan for when you want to start this process in the middle of a year.

Figure 1.3 shows two additional rows than on the basic plan. Both plans start with the current year's sales goal; Figure 1.3 takes into account the fact that a portion of the year has elapsed. Of course, as with any planning tool, you will have to refine your approach over several years of testing your assumptions and building in seasonal or other variations.

FIGURE 1.2 **Prospecting Business Plan Model**

Current year's sales goal	
Average sales size ($50K)	
Sales required (sales goal ÷ average sales size)	
Opportunities required (sales required × 3)	
Meetings required (opportunities required × 2)	
Completed calls required (meetings required × 4)	
Dials (CCs required × 4)	
Dials/day (dials ÷ 250)	

FIGURE 1.3 Prospecting Business Plan—Mid-year Implementation

Current year's sales goal	
Less: year-to-date sales	
"To Go" sales goal	
Average sales size ($50K)	
Sales required (sales goal ÷ average sales size)	
Opportunities required (sales required × 3)	
Meetings required (opportunities required × 2)	
Completed calls required (meetings required × 4)	
Dials (CCs required × 4)	
Dials/day (dials ÷ 250)	

To use the prospecting business plan, deduct your sales to date from the current year's sales goal to determine your sales goal for the remainder of the year. We call this the "To Go" sales goal. Then divide the "To Go" sales goal by the average sales size. If you do not know this figure, you should be able to get it from your sales manager. If your manager does not have this information either, make an educated estimate. The remainder of Figure 1.3 is the same as Figure 1.2, so just following the instructions in Figure 1.3 to complete the remainder of your Prospecting Business Plan.

Now, an Example

Figure 1.4 illustrates the process by way of example. In Figure 1.4, we start with a sales goal for the year of $1 million. Sales to date, to the point of implementation, are $250,000. This gives us a "To Go" sales goal of $750,000.

FIGURE 1.4 Prospecting Business Plan—Mid-year Implementation, Actual Example

Current year's sales goal	$1,000,000
Less: year-to-date sales	250,000
"To Go" sales goal	750,000
Average sales size ($50K)	50,000
Sales required (sales goal ÷ average sales size)	15
Opportunities required (sales required × 3)	45
Meetings required (opportunities required × 2)	90
Completed calls required (meetings required × 4)	360
Dials (CCs required × 4)	1,440
Dials/day (dials ÷ number of selling days left in year)	8

Assuming that the average sales size in this example is $50,000, this means you must make 15 sales during the remainder of the year to reach the annual sales goal. Next, multiply the number of sales required by 3 to come up with the number of opportunities required to reach your sales goal. That is, in my consulting work, I have found that a closing ratio of 33 percent—or one out of every three valid opportunities—is a reliable starting point for estimating your closing ratio. Using the ratio of three opportunities to one closed sale, you will need 45 opportunities to gain the 15 sales required to reach your "To Go" sales goal.

Of course, in your company, the closing ratio may be different, so you can go to your manager and ask what the company's historical sales data suggests, then use this as your closing ratio instead. Always use internal company data where available, though the 3-to-1 ratio here has proven reliable after many years of research and the experience of many thousands of sales people. Remember that, no matter what ratio you use, you should periodically compare it to your actual results and refine your approach to determine your true sales ratio.

Next, you calculate the number of new opportunity meetings you need to have to meet your sales goal. A new opportunity meeting is the first meeting you have with a customer or prospect that has the potential to yield a new opportunity. As you know, once a new opportunity is identified, it may take additional meetings to close the sale. In this context, the second, third, even tenth meetings regarding the same opportunity are not counted; only the first meeting counts as a new opportunity meeting. In this sample plan, the requirement is 90 meetings, based on a meeting-to-opportunity ratio of 2 to 1. That is, for every two meetings you have, one will result in a new opportunity.

The ratio is close here because a customer or prospect generally entertains a sales meeting for one reason only: to meet an unfilled need. When the potential customer invites you to a meeting based on an unfilled need, you have a relatively high chance that a sales opportunity will result from that meeting.

Note that this does not suggest you will close the sale. Rather, you have about a 50 percent chance of identifying a new sales opportunity. You then need to follow through on the opportunity with additional meetings. Ultimately, you will arrive at the point of sale, and this is the point at which you win the one-sale-out-of-three opportunities that characterizes the example. So, in this example, 90 new opportunity meetings are required to reach the "To Go" sales goal.

The next step is to consider the completed calls. A "completed call" is when you pick up the phone (i.e., when making a prospecting call) and speak to the person you intended to reach. If your intent is to speak with the vice president of human resources at XYZ Company, that vice president actually says hello to you. Leaving a message on the voice mail or speaking to the administrative assistant does not count as a completed call. However, if you do leave a message, and the vice president calls you back, that is considered a completed call. Again, you must have had direct, voice communication in order to count a phone call as a completed call.

The plan uses a 4 to 1 ratio of completed calls to meetings. I have worked with companies where this ratio is higher, but for purposes of illustration here, I use this ratio. If you work for a global company like IBM, Microsoft, AT&T, Coke, or Pepsi, your ratio of completed calls to meetings will likely be higher than if you worked at the local office-supply store. The brand recognition provided to the sellers by these global giants elevates the ratio in your favor—their very names open doors for you.

Now, based on that 4-to-1 ratio, you will need to have 360 completed calls to get 90 meetings. These 90 meetings will then yield 45 opportunities, and 45 opportunities will result in 15 sales. These 15 sales, at approximately $50,000 each, allow you to reach your "To Go" sales goal for the year.

The second-to-last step in the process is to calculate the number of dials you need to make to get 360 completed calls. In our example, I use a dial-to-completed-call ratio of 4-1. This result is a function of the time of the day when you call (there are better times and there are worse times to prospect) and also of the quality of the script you use or the message you leave. A weak script will yield poorer results while a polished one, with a strong value proposition, can achieve better than average results. The return ratio here is impacted by the brand recognition of your company as well. A seller in a global marketplace with a high-recognition name will likely outperform a seller for a local, nonbranded business, all other things being equal.

In this example, you will have to make 1,440 dials over the course of the remaining year to reach your sales goal. But first let's define what is meant by a dial.

A dial (of the phone) is the act of picking up the phone and dialing the number of the person you are trying to reach. The phone number can be a direct dial number or the general company number, as long as you can theoretically reach the person you want to reach. Additionally, the phone must ring! Only then can you record the activity of making one prospecting "dial." That means "busy" signals don't count.

Also, a prospecting dial—as opposed to another type of dial—must have the objective of setting up a meeting, either face to face or on the telephone. As you might expect, the meeting cannot be just any meeting, however. It must be a new opportunity meeting, meaning it must have at least the potential of generating a new sales opportunity.

Ultimately, what Figure 1.4 is demonstrating is the number of prospecting dials you need to make to reach your annual and/or "To Go" sales goal. As Figure 1.4 shows, this number of required dials is going to be large. The final step in this process is to calculate the number of dials per day that you need to make to reach that large total. So, the final step is to divide the total dials (900, in our case) by the remaining days in the year. As you know, there are four quarters to the sales year, and each quarter contains 13 weeks (52 weeks in the year divided by four quarters). There are also five days in a week, so to calculate the required dials per day, you first need to figure out how many days are left in the year.

Assume that you have completed the first quarter of the year, with three quarters to go. Since each quarter contains 13 weeks, there are 39 weeks left in the year, or 195 days. Divide the 1,440 calls by the 195 days and you have a result of approximately seven prospecting dials per day. Actually, the calculation yields

7.4 prospecting dials per day, but since you cannot make 40 percent of a prospecting call, round off any fractional values even if the fraction is less than 50 percent to the next greatest whole number. In our example, instead of making 7.4 dials per day, you would make 8 dials per day. More dials will result in more income for you over the long run.

And let me make one more important point: consistency is preferred to urgency. There is a big difference between making five dials per day for five consecutive days and making 25 dials on one day per week. Let's take a closer look at what we mean.

First, if you have ever tried to diet and lose weight, you probably found out that you cannot lose that weight by dieting only one day per week and then eating what you want on the other days. Consistency is always preferred to urgency. Likewise, if you have ever tried to work out to get into shape, you have discovered that you cannot work out one day per week and expect to be in great physical condition. Consistency is always preferred to urgency.

Second, if you leave all (or most) of your calls for one day during the week, especially Friday, you find too many unplanned activities will arise that will take you away from making your calls. Leaving your calls for the last day of the week, or trying to make all of your calls on one day per week, is a relatively risky implementation strategy.

Remember that the ratios used here are of little consequence because you will soon have your own ratios to work with. You can use these as a starting point until you get enough data (i.e., have made enough prospecting calls) to know what ratios are meaningful for you.

Final Thoughts

Congratulations! You have your first planning tool. It is called your prospecting business plan. Use this plan to determine the number of prospecting dials you will have to make each workday in order to reach your sales goals by the end of the year. You have this plan for two specific reasons:

1. To ensure that you always reach your sales goal. After all, this is the most important reason a company hires sales professionals in the first place.

2. To eliminate the selling peaks and valleys that plague most sales professionals. There is no need to experience selling peaks and valleys, so long as you make a fixed and measurable investment in the prospecting process. And when I tell you to make a fixed and measurable daily investment (of five dials per day, in our example), I mean daily, not weekly.

Remember that salespeople tend to overinvest in opportunity management and underinvest in prospecting. This, in and of itself, will keep you from realizing your full potential in the field of sales. It may even be sufficient to ruin your sales career.

Remember also that your prospecting business plan is based on a number of estimates and assumptions. It is up to you to re-evaluate your performance on a quarterly basis. Start with the full-year plan presented in Figure 1.2 for the first quarter, and then use the mid-year implementation in Figures 1.3 and 1.4 for the remaining three quarters.

Also, you do not have to wait until the end of the quarter to do your evaluation. Sales quarters are made up of three sales months, and sales months are made up of four sales weeks, so you can use any of these smaller periods to assess your prospecting business plan. The longer you wait into the year, the more difficult it will be to adjust the plan.

In the next chapter, I introduce your next sales planning tool: your territory plan.

Territory Plans
The Heart of the Sales Planning Process

The territory plan is the crown jewel of the sales planning process. When you consider your options for increasing your sales, there are only two ways to accomplish that result. The first is to find new customers—this is why I gave you the prospecting business plan in the prior chapter. With this plan you invest appropriately in the new business development or prospecting process. The second way to grow sales is to sell more to your existing customers. We are going to discuss this part of your sales strategy in the next chapter when we discuss Account Planning.

In a sense, the implication of the prospecting business plan is that prospecting is simply a numbers game. However, that's not really the case, so I follow the prospecting business plan with the territory plan. Indeed, there is quite a bit more to prospecting than just determining the number of proactive, outbound new-business-development calls that you make on a daily basis. So, the second key element of your sales strategy to obtain new customers is your territory plan, which will be discussed later in this chapter.

I don't mean to imply here that prospecting is limited to finding new customers. You can also prospect to existing customers and expand an existing relationship. This is the second way to grow your sales—to sell more products or services to your existing customers.

For example, suppose you have a customer with two divisions, a wholesale one and a retail one. Also assume that you do business with the retail division. You can leverage your relationship with the retail division by prospecting to expand that relationship into the wholesale division. Likewise, account planning, which is discussed in Chapter 3, is not limited to existing customers. If you have a large potential customer in your territory, you can develop an account plan that will increase your chances of penetrating that new account.

But, with the understanding that prospecting can be used to both obtain new customers and expand existing customer relationships, and the recognition that account planning can be used to both expand existing customer relationships and open new accounts, we can turn our focus to the territory planning process. Indeed, the territory plan is the heart of the sales planning process. This is because your prospecting business plan and your account plans provide the details you need to execute your territory plan. In a sense, the territory plan is like the entrepreneur's or CEO's business plan. It is the document and strategy that allow you to achieve your sales goal. And that, of course, is what selling is all about.

The Large-Account Strategy

There are two types of sellers in the field. The first is the large-account seller; the second is the territory seller.

The *large-account seller* will have one, or a few, large accounts that make up the individual's customer/prospect base. My favorite example of a large account is General Electric. If you were to study General Electric from a sales perspective, you would find that it has between 150 and 200 operating companies. Each of these companies can have multiple buying centers, in different regions of the world (the Americas, Europe, the Middle East and Africa, and Asia Pacific). So, even though you have only one account to work with, when you take the time to break down this account into its operating companies and buying centers, you would have plenty of "subaccounts" to work with.

There's a big sales myth to be dispelled here. It is said that working with a large account, or a small set of large accounts, is very different from working with a large number of smaller accounts. In reality, these two situations have more in common than usually assumed. From a territory-management perspective, they are quite similar.

The second type of seller, the *territory seller,* often has a relatively large number of accounts and these accounts are typically smaller and often located in a specified geographic region. Territory sellers often face a significant challenge: how to prioritize or systematize their work with these accounts so as to maximize results in a limited time frame.

Actually, how to prioritize your set of accounts is one of the most significant sales issues you will have to address. This is a challenge faced by both territory sellers and large-account sellers. The only difference is that territory sellers work with accounts, whereas large-account sellers work most often with subaccounts or components of large companies. So, again, the problems and challenges of these two different types of sellers are very similar, and both can benefit from the overall territory planning process that I have deemed the "large-account strategy."

The Large-Account Strategy in Action

When I started my first company in 1983, it was part of the high-growth computer-training industry, and the industry sat right smack in the middle of the technology boom that characterized the 1980s and 1990s. As went technology, so went our industry and so went my company.

At the point I sold the company in 1995, I had about 400 sales professionals throughout the United States and Canada. Starting when I had only 100 field sellers, I maintained a sales ladder, ranking the sales people from number 1 (most sales during the year) on down the ladder (least annual sales). As I did the ranking over the years, I noticed an interesting trend. It was as if we had two classes of sellers. First, there were always three sales people who outsold the rest of the company, year in and year out. And then there were the rest of the sales people. The difference between the top three and the remaining ones was considerable. It was as if only these three sellers could be at the top of the list. The order of the three top performers would change from year to year, it was as if there were an elite club with a membership limited to these three selling superstars.

This situation presented an interesting opportunity to study why these three sellers had become so exceptional. We brought them in from the field to learn why they consistently outperformed the rest of the organization. By the end of the week, we had the answer. Individually, they said the secret to their success was a large-account strategy, and they proceeded to show why this strategy was so powerful.

The Secret of Sales Success

Take a moment to study Figure 2.1 because it reveals the secret to sales success: the large-account strategy. In this figure, we

FIGURE 2.1 The Secret of Top Performers

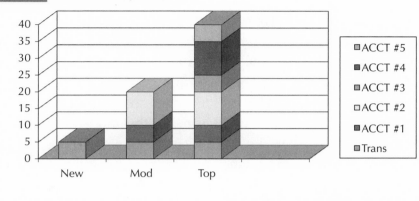

start with the familiar three categories of sales professionals—new, moderate, and top. The three categories simply reflect each sales professional's current opportunity workload—that is, the new sales professional is managing a relatively low level of current opportunities. This group title is no reflection of age or tenure with a company; you may be a 20-year sales veteran experiencing a terrible sales slump and could well be in this category. The moderate sales professional has a current opportunity workload of moderate size, and the top sales professional has a current opportunity workload very high relative to his or her peers.

You can see that the sales for the new category are very low. This is what you would expect, but it is the *composition* of those sales that provides us with some insight here. That is, the sales of a seller in the new category tend to be transactional in nature—small and with no pattern of predictability. The new sales person cannot count on a particular customer to give more than one order during the current sales year.

In the moderate category, you notice that the sales volume

increases. But what is more interesting here is how the increase occurs. Moderate sellers still have a transactional component to their revenue base (in fact, all sellers always have a transactional element to their revenue base), and that transactional element allows these sellers to develop future large accounts. However, sellers in this category have a second component—a relationship or large-account factor. In Figure 2.1, the moderate seller has two large accounts in the current customer set.

Before proceeding further, I need to explain what I mean by a large account. There are three factors to a large account: individual sales are significant (there can be some small individual sales, but most tend to be large), total sales are significant, and sales recur throughout the year. Recurring sales means that the customer buys from time and time throughout the year, without the sales person having to resell each transaction. What this means is that the sales of the moderate seller start to form a predictable pattern.

From a time-management perspective, this predictable pattern represents a breakthrough. Getting that first sale from an account is a time-consuming process—you have to work hard to demonstrate that the risk of doing business with a new supplier is worth bearing, especially if they have been doing business with your competition, who may be servicing the account quite well and for some time now.

By way of example, let's assume that you are a sales professional working at the local office-supply store. Let's also assume that you just landed one of the larger companies in the town as your new customer. This new account will place its first order and then eventually use up the stationery and office supplies that they purchased. If you did a good job servicing the account during the first sale, the buyer will place a second order when goods are needed. That second purchase will require little work from you, especially when you compare it to the work required to get the first order. In fact, the customer likely will just call and place the order. The buyer may even place the order with a sales assistant in your department or perhaps on the company's Web site or portal.

The good news is that future orders from this customer will continue to be relatively easy to execute. The better news is that the customer will likely continue to order, under the assumption that your company continues to do a good job servicing the account. The buyer may even continue to order beyond the first year if you have done an exceptional job servicing the account. In short, your large account will provide a revenue stream with relatively little sales effort on your part. You are now free to develop additional large accounts over time. An increasing number of large accounts will move the moderate seller to the top seller category. Hence, if you want to be a top performer, you must develop a significant number (five to ten) of large accounts. However, this, in and of itself, is not the large-account strategy.

How the Large-Account Strategy Works

Let us assume that you are a territory account manager and your territory is the entire state of New York. This is your first day on the job and this is also a new territory for your company. Where do you start? What accounts do you call on?

Setting up a territory in an effective manner is where sellers often make significant mistakes. In fact, this can mean the difference between a successful sales career and a moderate or less than successful one. As I mentioned, my first company had three outstanding sellers, and their success was a direct result of their having effectively established their respective sales territories. Similarly, some companies severely limit their effectiveness by not establishing and deploying proper sales territories. Not only does this limit their selling success but it also costs millions, and possibly hundreds of millions, of dollars per year through duplication of sales efforts.

Some Common Mistakes in Setting Up Your Territory

Before getting into how best to establish the sales territories, taking a look at some common mistakes can be helpful.

❑ *The practice run.* Perhaps the most dramatic and recurring mistake that is made is to do what I like to call the "practice run." This is when a seller decides to start working with the smaller accounts in the market first; the thinking is to use these accounts to fine-tune the approach. The problem is that these sellers view the accounts as the less significant ones in their territory and thus aren't as concerned about the outcome. They believe that once their sales process is optimized, they can move on to the larger accounts. This approach is in direct violation of the large-account strategy, however.

Remember, your most precious commodity as a sales professional is time. You must treat time with the same care as you do your personal money. Wasting time is akin to wasting money, and working with smaller accounts before you have fully worked the larger accounts in your territory is the single largest time-waster in the world of professional sales.

❑ *The random walk.* Another common mistake is to let your current opportunities drive your account selection—a situation I call the "random walk." To meet quarterly sales goals, especially in publicly held companies, sellers often focus too much on current revenue production to the detriment of long-term success. In practice, the seller always moves to the next most likely transaction to close, ignoring the need to develop the large-account relationships farther back in the pipeline. In the short run, it seems the seller is doing well, however, ultimately that seller won't achieve significant market share.

❏ *The fast-food approach.* Have you ever noticed how fast-food restaurants congregate near one another? What happens is that one company—say, McDonald's—spends millions of dollars in research to find the busiest intersections in a given area. Once McDonald's places its stake in the ground, Wendy's and Burger King, direct competitors, follow suit by locating on opposite or adjacent street corners. They leverage the investment made by McDonald's to find where the most customers are likely to be.

Unfortunately, sellers tend to ignore the obvious and not learn from the experiences of industry leaders. In fact, in sales we tend to do just the opposite!

Now, of these three types of mistakes, let's look further at the last one. Suppose we are in a market that is relatively new to us, or in a market where the company does not have much of a presence. We start by calling on a few of the larger accounts, only to find out that they are already doing business with the competition. At this point, we tend to target the smaller accounts, reasoning that the competition is busy with the larger accounts.

To begin, you may want to consider why your competition is not working with the smaller accounts. The reason is that they have already learned, like McDonald's did in our example, where the best customers are. In this case, the best customers are the larger accounts—the ones that the competition already has. Thus, getting these larger accounts must be the major component of your sales strategy.

Why the Large-Account Strategy Works

These three examples of mistakes ignore the key element of the large-account strategy: work with the larger accounts in the market. This strategy is crucial to success, as shown by those top three sellers in my company. But perhaps the largest impediment to implementing this strategy is the fact that it is counterintuitive. After all, why wouldn't you want to practice on the smaller accounts first? Why wouldn't you want to follow the opportunity trail and limit the rejections you receive? And why wouldn't you want to find some new accounts where the competition has not already heavily penetrated?

The reason is that the large-account strategy works! It might seem to make sense to polish your approach before you set out to penetrate the larger accounts, but that's not true. It might seem better to capture the easiest sales because they promise immediate reward, but that's not true. It might seem better to not tackle your competition for those larger accounts, but that's not true, either.

Our experience in sales has proved that the large-account strategy works best. In addition to helping our own company in a significant way, we have implemented the strategy at a number of our clients, including a global financial services company, a global technology company, and small- and medium-size businesses. In every case, the large-account strategy changed the way they approached the market and generated significant productivity gains and revenue enhancements.

Implementing the Large-Account Strategy

It should come as no surprise to hear that large accounts typically come from large prospects. Remember that one of the key elements of a large account is its ability to provide an ongoing, significant revenue stream. And what type of company is most likely to support an ongoing revenue stream?

Large accounts will most likely come from large prospects. Yes, it is possible that a small prospect can become a large account. And it is possible that a large prospect will *not* become a large account. However, on average, the larger prospects are more likely to become the larger accounts in your customer base. For example, who has a greater need for office supplies from the sales person at the office-supply store—IBM, a global corporation with more than 300,000 employees, or a CPA who works out of his home?

Take the Measure of Your Prospects

To begin implementing your large-account strategy you need to select a method of measuring the buying potential of the companies (i.e., prospects) in your market. For example, if you are selling sales training, as I do, you might determine the size of a company by researching its total revenues (or gross sales or total turnover) for the year. Total revenue is an indication of the size of the prospect's sales force, and the larger the sales force, the more likely they will need sales training. Most important, if the target company has a large sales organization, it will likely be able to purchase a larger amount of sales training, on an ongoing basis, so that the account can be a large one over time.

If you are selling software, on the other hand, a good estimate of buying potential might be the number of employees in the company. The larger the company, the more likely it will need software. Also, because software is typically sold on a per-user basis, the more employees a company has, the more software those employees will require for given applications.

To get company employee counts or total revenues, you could go to a resource such as Hoovers (www.hoovers.com) and obtain a ranked listing of all companies in the state. This takes about five minutes (i.e., it is easy to obtain) and is available at a reasonable cost (annual subscription fee). If you don't want to pay for a resource such as Hoovers, there are typically free resources that rank companies similarly. Some of these free or relatively free resources can be found on the Internet, from local chambers of commerce, or in business publications such as *Crain's* for cities such as New York, Chicago, or Detroit.

The problem with low-cost or free resources is that they provide very little additional information. Hoovers, on the other hand, offers a vast wealth of information that is all useful at various stages in the sales cycle. This means you will usually spend much more time obtaining free resources than you will by purchasing a subscription to Hoovers.

In most industries, these two general measurements—revenues and employee numbers—work quite well in estimating prospects. However, certain industries may have more specific measurements. For example, one of our clients is a publishing company (i.e., they sell advertising space in their magazines). A good measure of buying potential in this instance might be a prospect's total advertising budget, an indication of how much income is being derived from the advertising that is being sold. Another client is a large airline; in this industry, a prospect's global travel budget might be a good measure of buying potential. Similarly, if you are selling to the retail industry, it is not uncommon to find companies ranked by the number of square feet of retail space they occupy. The more square footage, the larger the buying potential.

In order to use an industry-specific measurement, that measurement must meet two important tests. First, the statistics must be easy to obtain. You can always get a list of companies ranked by employee count or total revenue; however, industry-specific measurements are often difficult and costly to obtain. Assuming that you can easily find an industry-specific measurement that is also relatively cost-effective, you must apply a second, more important test. Is the list is as comprehensive as that provided by Hoovers or a similar resource? By comparison, industry-specific resources are often incomplete.

Most lists, whether industry-specific or not, always cover the top end of the market relatively well. For example, in a list of New York businesses, you would find companies like IBM, Citigroup, and Verizon at the top of the list. These companies are so well known that it hardly takes a list to remember to include them in your large-account strategy. But what you find only 31 companies down the Hoovers list for New York is a company named Volt Information Services. Volt has over $2 billion in annual sales and approximately 46,000 employees worldwide. This is a relatively large company, yet one that may not be included on other resource lists. Volt is not as well known, and would make a great account for anyone reading this book. The next 70 accounts on the list are likewise not as well known and may be omitted from more industry-specific resources.

In short, if you are not aware of a company, you cannot include it in your sales territory. To make matters worse, if you are not selling to some of the larger accounts in your territory, you will be selling to the smaller accounts, and selling to smaller accounts when there are larger accounts to be had is a violation of the large-account strategy. You will be allocating your time in a less than optimal way and your sales results will be suboptimal as a result. You will be running the risk of not maximizing the value you can receive from the accounts in your sales territory. You will not be able to sell up to your potential because you will not be spending your time with the very best prospects.

If you extend this behavior beyond one account, you will have created almost a random territory plan. For example, Volt would not be the only company missing from your territory plan. So, the first step in creating a strong territory plan is to have a firm understanding of the accounts in the market.

What if I Don't Work at the Top End of a Market?

There are many companies that target what is known as the "middle market" and there are still other companies that target small businesses. Also, many large companies such as IBM and PricewaterhouseCoopers look toward the small-business and middle-market companies for growth these days. Likewise, in Asia and in emerging markets, such as Brazil and Russia, the top end of the market is very small. As a result, the entire market is more closely focused on small and medium business (SMB) types.

In fact, the SMB marketplace is very important to sales professionals in today's sales environment. You can implement the large-account strategy just as easily in an SMB market as you can in a large-account market. In fact, if you work in the middle market or at the lower end of the market, you will find the large-account strategy works very well. As with top market performers, you assess the accounts in the market and rank them according to buying potential, most efficiently by using one of the two metrics discussed above—gross sales or number of employees.

When you are working at the top end of the market, with companies like IBM and Citigroup, you run the risk of missing companies like Volt Information Services. However, when you go to the middle market and the lower end of the market, none of the companies you will be approaching have a globally recognizable brand. Avoid presuming a poor view of the market, lest that lead you to inefficient allocation of your major sales resource—your time.

Determine Your Account Load

Once you have a comprehensive listing of the accounts in the market and have ranked them according to buying potential, start at the top of the list and select a reasonable number of accounts to work with. What is reasonable, of course, will depend on the size of the account (i.e., is the account a global corporation with many business units, or is the account a smaller company with only one business unit?) and the stage of your sales development (i.e., new, moderate, or top).

I can't tell you how many accounts you can manage at one time, but I can tell you that a new account manager will be able to handle quite a number more than a moderate account manager. I can also tell you that a moderate account manager can handle quite few more than a top account manager.

Referring again to Figure 2.1, you'll see that a new account manager has no large-account relationships. There will be some transactional relationships and many accounts will simply be prospecting relationships. Since a prospecting relationship is nothing more than calling up the account to establish a meeting, you can handle quite a few of these at this stage.

However, when you move to the moderate category, you develop several large-account relationships. The large-account relationships will diminish your capacity to have prospecting relationships. Likewise, when you move from the moderate category to the top category, the number of large-account relationships increases yet again and the number of prospecting relationships diminishes.

The 80/20 Rule to Estimate Territory Size

I'm sure that you are familiar with the 80/20 rule, which for sales professionals tells us that 80 percent of our revenue or total sales for the year will come from 20 percent of the accounts in our territory plan.

However, the 80/20 rule holds true only if you are a top account manager. A top account manager's sales will always reflect the 80/20 rule because they have enough large accounts to make up 80 percent of their sales; the remainder of their sales, the 20 percent, come from the remaining accounts in their list. Now, let's see how we can use the 80/20 rule to put the finishing touches on our large-account strategy and the territory plan.

Let us assume that you are a top account manager and your sales mirror the 80/20 rule. Let's also assume you have eight large accounts. (A top account manager will typically have between six and ten large accounts.) If you have eight accounts that make up 80 percent of your sales, how many accounts make up the remaining 20 percent? In case your math skills are a bit rusty, the answer is 40 (eight accounts divided by 20 percent, or 0.20). One could estimate, therefore, that a top account manager can effectively manage a total account list of approximately 50 accounts.

Working backward, we can now look at the moderate account manager. Assume that the moderate account manager has four large accounts. (The number of large accounts for a moderate account manager can range from two or three to about five or six, but no more.) The sales probably reflect a ratio of 70 to 30, large accounts to transactional revenue, or perhaps 60 to 40.

With the number of large accounts at four, the moderate account manager could, therefore, manage twice the number of prospects. We had approximately 40 prospects for the top account manager, so we can safely double that for the moderate account manager. In sum, a moderate account manager can handle approximately 80 to 100 accounts.

Finally, the new account manager could handle approximately 300 accounts, assuming the individual had one large account and the number of transactional accounts for the moderate account manager was multiplied by 4. Accordingly, the new account manager could handle, say, 300 accounts. In this way, you know how many accounts you can handle.

Note: if you are in doubt as to the number of accounts that you should have on your list, err on the low side. It is much easier to add accounts later on if you have excess time than it is to remove accounts, especially after you have made contact with them. It will make you appear less professional in their eyes.

Create the Account List

Now, you need to create the optimal account list. You start, for example, at the top of a list of companies such as provided by Hoovers and count down the number of accounts suggested for your category of sales professional. This way, you are working with the top end of your market, having done your due diligence to ensure that these are the correct accounts for your market segment.

As an example, let's take a look at Figure 2.2, which is a sample territory plan. Typically, you list all of your large accounts in the left column. (Remember: a large account is one that provides both significant and recurring revenue.) These are your customers and you will use your account plans (discussed

FIGURE 2.2 **Your Territory Plan**

Top Accounts	Top Prospects
Account 1	Prospect Company 1
Account 2	Prospect Company 2
Account 3	Prospect Company 3
Account 4	Prospect Company 4
	Prospect Company 5
	Prospect Company 6
	Prospect Company 7
	Prospect Company 8
	Prospect Company 9
	Prospect Company 10

in the next chapter) to grow those account relationships and expand your account penetration.

In the right column, you list your top ten prospects. (Your top prospects are those on your account list that are not already large accounts.) Your goal is to move one account at a time from the right-hand column to the left-hand column—until your sales from large accounts mirrors the 80/20 rule. At this point, you will be a top account manager.

If you are starting as a new account manager, with no large accounts, you have nothing in the left-hand column but you have your top ten prospects in the right-hand column. You will work all of these accounts on your prospects list, putting special emphasis on the ten on your territory plan. Once you have that first large account, you place it in the left-hand column and fill that empty slot in the right-hand column with the next largest account on your prospects list. You continue to repeat the process to move from new to moderate and ultimately to top account manager.

Going from Here

If you recall, I mentioned that you could easily implement the territory plan to have an immediate and significant impact on your sales career. This entails selecting a demographic that best measures the buying potential in your business (such as total sales at the company or employee account at the company) and then using a resource such as Hoovers to obtain a comprehensive list of the companies (or individuals, if you sell into the consumer market) in your market, ranked by buying potential.

I provided guidelines for judging how many accounts should be on your list. You start at the top end of your market (which could be the top of the list if you are selling to large accounts or it could be somewhere in the middle of the list if you are selling to middle-market accounts) and count down the number of accounts you require. This is now your account list and you are set up to implement the large-account strategy as part of your territory plan.

There are two final points that I wish to make. First, you should always have ten accounts on your top prospect list. Why? Because unless you have 100 percent market share in your target market, there will always be more prospects to work. And you will be working these prospects in the order suggested by the large-account strategy.

Second, you do not stop working once your sales mirror the 80/20 rule. In sales, you never stop working, because there is no stable state in sales. Either you are growing your market share or your competition is! Unfortunately, we are entitled only a little bit of time to "smell the roses" before we must get back to the work of serving customer needs.

With that thought in mind, let's move on to the next chapter, and learn how to develop and grow account relationships with good account plans.

CHAPTER 3

Account Plans
The Third Leg of the Triple Crown

In the United States, there is a series of three horse races each year to determine if there's a three-year-old horse that can reach the pinnacle of horse racing: winning the Triple Crown. The first race is the Kentucky Derby, the second is the Preakness Stakes, and the third is the Belmont Stakes. Each race is at a different location and is a different length, requiring the horse to excel at three different lengths. Since 1919, only 11 horses have won the Triple Crown.

When I think about account planning, I imagine the Triple Crown. As with the Triple Crown in horse racing, sales people have three different tools—the prospecting business plan, the territory plan, and the account plan—and each tool has its own purpose. Like the Triple Crown, making all three tools work in concert is rare, but the reward if you succeed is that you rise to the top of your profession.

Your Account Plan

As with the prospecting and territory plans, I am not providing the most sophisticated and comprehensive process here. Instead, I give you one or two high-impact, easy-to-implement ideas to get your selling career off to a flying start. If you are a field-tested veteran experiencing a slump, these ideas will revive your career and help you assume your former position in the profession.

There are two types of account plans: those for existing customers (typically large accounts) and those for prospects (designed to migrate these accounts to customer status). The formats of these plans should be and are exactly the same. However, the detail in a plan for an existing customer is different from that of one for a new prospect, given that you have a lot more information about your customers.

How Many Account Plans Should You Maintain?

Figure 2.2 in Chapter 2 was a sample territory plan showing four large accounts and ten top prospects. I recommend that you maintain an account plan for each of your top accounts.

As you can see if you refer back to that figure, there was space on the form for up to ten large accounts. Since your large accounts represent a large percentage of your revenue—over 50 percent and up to 80 percent—it is appropriate to invest in the account-planning process, as well as to strategize about defending the accounts from the competition, and how to grow the existing account relationships.

What About Prospects?

Your ten top prospects are also very important. To become a top-performing account manager, you need to turn prospects into customers. As part of your large-account strategy, you will place emphasis on the ten prospects listed in your territory plan.

These are the largest prospects in your territory at a given point in time, and your account plans for these prospects will help you optimize your sales results. If you can turn these prospects into large accounts, they will have the greatest impact on your business.

I don't mean to imply that you should not welcome other accounts. You most certainly will. What I do mean is that the largest prospects will have the greatest impact on your sales when you convert these accounts into customers. That's why I recommend that you also maintain account plans for each of your top ten prospects.

What About the Workload?

You may be concerned about being able to maintain four large account plans and ten prospect plans, as indicated in Figure 2.2. That is a genuine concern, especially considering the fact that your number of large accounts will grow over time and your number of prospects will stay at ten throughout the process. This represents a heavy workload.

In Chapter 2, I discussed workload with respect to your large accounts. Since four large accounts represent 80 percent of your total revenue, some planning and strategizing is in order. However, handling your prospects also requires some planning and strategizing. After all, these prospects will be your large accounts of tomorrow.

Keep in mind that the account plans for your prospects will be smaller than those for your customers. Probably two or three, or even four, prospecting account plans will equal one large-customer account plan, in terms of information contained. So, while ten account plans for your prospects seems like a lot, it is not. To summarize, the recommendation is to maintain an account plan for each account in your territory plan.

The Account Development Cycle

Any account plan comprises two key elements: an account development cycle and a comprehensive sales discovery process. Understanding the account development cycle helps you set realistic goals for developing your account relationships. Having a comprehensive view of the purchasing procedures, gained via a sales discovery process, helps you navigate the customer's system for buying goods and services. We begin by looking at the account development cycle. The sales discovery process is discussed in Chapter 5.

All too often, sales people try to skip the nine steps of the account development cycle, instead speeding through the sales process. While it is possible to skip some steps in the cycle, success in these instances is clearly the exception, not the rule. So let's take a look at the steps in the account development cycle. They are presented in Figure 3.1.

FIGURE 3.1 **The Account Development Cycle**

1. Identify the customer's needs.
2. Start to position your company relative to the customer's needs.
3. Gain your first small sale.
4. Gain additional small sales.
5. Gain your first large sale.
6. Gain additional large sales.
7. Become the primary provider.
8. Expand your account penetration.
9. Earn trusted adviser status.

Identify Customer Needs and Position Yourself

As the figure shows, the first step in the cycle is to understand the customer's or prospect's needs. Without a firm understanding of the customer's needs, it is impossible to build a lasting account relationship. It is possible to make a sale without understanding the customer's needs (though even that is not likely), but remember that you are not only interested in making a sale. You are interested in building this prospect into a large account—one with significant and recurring revenue. Since understanding the customer's needs is one of the most important things you do as a sales professional, Chapter 5 is devoted to that needs assessment, termed the sales discovery process.

The next step is to position yourself, your company, and your solution relative to the customer's needs. In all likelihood, the customer is going to buy the solution that the customer best believes suits the needs. So, positioning is another important topic, and again it is deferred to Chapter 5, where the sales discovery process is discussed.

Start with Small Sales

Sometimes a good example is the best way to put a point across. Here's a personal experience to illustrate how the account development cycle can be put to work for you, especially with regard to starting small and steadily building an account, which is step three in the account development cycle.

Getting Your Foot in the Door. When I was running our computer training company back in the early 1990s, we had an opportunity to be part of the Merck vendor-selection process. Winning the Merck account, which is a giant pharmaceutical company headquartered in the United States, would be a great accomplishment, perhaps the greatest sale I ever made. How we won the Merck account is a great illustration of successful use of the account development cycle.

In 1992, our company was excited to receive an invitation to be part of the Merck RFP (Request for Proposal) process. RFPs are typically issued by larger companies like Merck when they are looking to make a major purchase. Here, Merck was seeking a provider for its computer-training needs in the United States. Our excitement soon faded, however, as we discovered there was an existing provider—one of our competitors had been working closely with Merck at least two years.

We had never done any business with Merck before. At the time, vendor consolidation was a big trend in corporate America and Merck maintained tight control over the contracts it issued. That meant that our competition was the current contract holder and Merck had done its best to ensure that all of its business went through, and not around, the corporate contract office. This new offer was to be a two-year agreement worth several million dollars.

If you were the procurement officer, would you issue a contract to a company Merck had never done business with? Responding to this RFP was going to be a time-consuming process for us, and since we had virtually no chance of winning, we told Merck we were not going to respond to the RFP. Because we were one of the major players in the industry, the procurement officer contacted us to find out why we dropped out and I told him. During the discussion, I discovered a current need that Merck had that the incumbent provider was not able to service. It was a very small need, but it resulted in our having the opportunity to deliver one computer training class at Merck.

We seized the opportunity for our first small sale. It was that "small sale," as noted in step three of the account development cycle that got us on our way to success in the Merck RFP process. To put this in perspective, imagine you were selling stationery and office supplies to Merck; our sale was the equivalent of selling one pencil or pen. And while we were excited to make the sale, we had to look at our position realistically: How much of a difference could one class or one small sale make?

We found out that it made a profound difference. Not only did we use the account development cycle to our advantage, making that small sale put us on the Merck approved-supplier list. And once we were on the list, it would be easier for Merck to buy from us. With the RFP process, we could now say that we had some (minimal) experience working with Merck, and we could say that the delivery of our first sale was a success. While that first sale was small, its implications were huge.

The need we filled was to deliver training on a new release of Microsoft Word. In the earlier days of the computer industry, software developers like Microsoft issued new releases of their desktop software quite frequently, and it was important to large companies like Merck that their personnel be trained on the latest versions. One of our strengths as a company was that we were consistently "first to market" with new training programs. When a new version of software was released, our training was ready before that of the competition. Merck's need for more training on this new version of Microsoft Word led to a few more small sales—step four of the cycle.

We were starting to establish a real track record at Merck. That small track record could be cited in the proposal process to enhance our chance in the RFP process. The beauty of this example is that it shows how you can start with small sales to break into an account that can lead to much greater sales. Many sales people skip the small sales and get right into larger sales at an account. By establishing a track record places you in a stronger situation when it comes to larger sales.

Helping Mitigate Risk. If the customer has never done business with you before, there is a significant risk, from their perspective, of starting to do business with you. The customer is aware of the level of service provided by an existing vendor and in all likelihood that is satisfactory. After all, if the customer weren't satisfied, that vendor would have been replaced.

There are only three ways a customer mitigates the risk of using a new vendor. The first is to start small, with that first small sale. That's why the account development cycle places step three, starting with small sales, near the beginning of the process. Continuing to increase the size of the sale from that point is almost a rule of nature.

The second way the customer mitigates risk is by seeking references. If you can provide examples of other companies you have worked with that are similar to this one, you will be closer to successfully completing a sale. The prospect gains comfort by speaking to others in the same position and who have had a successful relationship with your company. Reference stories are discussed further in Chapter 8.

The final way a prospect mitigates risk is by seeking a guarantee. If you can offer a 100 percent, no-questions-asked, money-back guarantee, you may win that account. I do not advocate making this type of offer until you have tried the other two steps; in fact, the small sales and the reference stories may well be sufficient. Offering a money-back guarantee may not result in a win-win relationship for your company and therefore should be your fall-back position, not your lead position.

Penetrating the New Accounts. Large sales do not happen by accident. That's why I provide the account development cycle. It is a proven process for winning sales at new accounts. It also is a proven process for developing and expanding new account relationships.

Some sales people try to penetrate a new account by asking the prospect if he or she is happy with the current supplier. But this is not a good question and not a good way to penetrate a new account. The answer will almost always be yes, he or she is satisfied with the current supplier

Another approach some try is to convince the customer to split the business. The argument is that both companies provide their best service, for fear of the other's appearing better—that the competition encourages better service. This is not a wise move, either. If you use this approach to penetrate a new customer account, the customer and/or next vendor can use the same approach against you. This limits your ability to grow the account over the long run.

A third way some try to penetrate a new account is to lower their price until that price is so low the customer has to do business with you. Unfortunately, this is not a wise move, either. A discount today sets a precedent for later sales. In fact, a discounted offer establishes a price ceiling for all future sales. If you give a customer a 50 percent discount in order to get the business, you are not going to make the next sale at list price.

To properly penetrate a new account, you must be adept at the sales discovery process, which is discussed in Chapter 5. You must find something that the customer needs that the customer doesn't already have. For example, Merck had a need for the new training very early in a product's life cycle. Our having the training materials and a program ready before the competition gave us the opportunity to offer Merck something it needed but did not already have from the competition.

Additionally, because Merck needed the training and because there were no comparable solutions, we could sell the product to Merck at a highly profitable price and still penetrate a new account. This is one of the major advantages of following the account development cycle. If you try to penetrate an account with a readily available product, you dramatically lower your price, or you offer to split the business, you will fail to get the prospect to seriously consider your offer. On the other hand, following the account development cycle, giving the customer something he or she doesn't already have, is a non-price-sensitive sales process and the only way to properly develop an account relationship.

The Move to Larger Sales

The Microsoft Word training programs that we were delivering at Merck were general, open-enrollment classes available to all employees. One of the people attending the classes was a word-processing specialist in the legal department because some features of the new version of Word were helpful in preparing legal documents.

Legal word processing involves producing some complex, specialized documents. Not everyone can deliver software training for this specialized word processing, but we had a trainer knowledgeable in both Word and legal word processing. Merck's incumbent provider, our competition, had developed its own program for the new version of Microsoft Word by this point, and that company was the likely firm to deliver this series of specialized programs. Yet, since this was going to be a relatively large project, and when the incumbent saw the expertise required, they decided to back off. However, since we had the expertise, we delivered the programs and successfully completed our first large sale to Merck.

It is important to note that we gained our first large sale not by lowering our price, nor by asking the customer if he was happy with the incumbent provider, nor by arguing to split the business among multiple vendors. Rather, we gave the customer something he needed that he did not already have—the only sound way to develop account relationships.

At this point, we were quite a bit better off than we were when we started. We had established a track record, and were now ready for the later steps of the account development cycle. When the RFP process actually started, we were given great access to Merck data so that we could gather as much evidence as possible. In fact, we implemented the sales discovery process, which is discussed later in this chapter and in greater detail in Chapter 5.

Through this comprehensive discovery process we were able to uncover a number of additional items that the customer needed, which it was not getting from the competition. We developed a business solution stacked with services that the customer did not already have and that could produce significant cost savings. We then went on to win the RFP process and unseat the incumbent provider. Winning the RFP process had taken us all the way through to step seven of the account development cycle.

The Primary Provider—But Not So Fast . . .

We were now the primary provider to Merck of all products and services that our company offered. Most sales people think that this is where the account development cycle ends. It is not. There are two more important steps in the cycle that must be taken.

Step eight of the account development cycle, "Expand Your

Account Penetration," implies that there is more to account development than just becoming the customer's primary provider. A company is ever changing and ever evolving. If you think about all of the changes that have occurred in business practices over the last ten years or so, it is quite staggering: the Internet, financial compliance laws such as Sarbanes-Oxley (caused by the collapse of several corporate institutions like Enron and WorldCom), "do-not-call" legislation protecting consumers from getting unwanted telephone solicitations, and such. Because of constant change in the business environment, companies must either adapt or perish. This means that your customers' needs are never ending and ever changing, too. Once you solve today's business problem, there is another, waiting right behind it. A sales person can never rest on his or her laurels or feel secure with prior successes.

Expand Your Account Penetration

Earlier, I discussed using the sales discovery process to discover ways that your customer's needs are not being met. Even though you are now the primary provider for your category of products or services, that customer will always have needs outside of what you offer. It is your job to find those new needs before the competition does. If you do, you will be "expanding your account penetration."

Also remember how early steps in the account development cycle helped you to penetrate an account and become the primary provider. Remember that the competition can use those same techniques to penetrate your customer. They will get their first small sale and then try to expand their account relationship over time.

So, largely through your account plan, you will continue to use the sales discovery process to find that next new need. You will always be expanding your account penetration, because this is the only true way to defend that account from the competition.

The Trusted Adviser

The final step of the account development cycle is to become a trusted adviser to the company. Because you have consistently been identifying new customer needs and have marshaled the resources of your company to meet those needs, you have raised the bar on customer expectations. If you have successfully met those customers' expectations—or surpassed them—you are likely to become the resource they regularly consult.

It takes a long time to get from step one of the cycle to this final step. You will have gone above and beyond the call of duty many times, and you will have helped the customer grow their business, trim costs, and become more successful. This final acknowledgment of your role in their company's success gives you the highest honor that can be earned by a sales professional.

From this point on, the company will treat you as if you are part of their organization. They will provide you with information that you've never been privy to before. And, in turn, you will process this information for them, providing even greater levels of success to your customer. At this point, also, your market share at the account will continue to grow. You will likely be the customer's first choice for any sales opportunity that falls within your company's areas of expertise. You have finally reached the top of the mountain, but, again, my advice is to never rest on your laurels. Remember that if you are not growing the account relationship, the competition most certainly is.

The Sales Discovery Process

The first account-planning strategy I mentioned at the beginning of this chapter was the account development cycle. But recall that I said there were two facets to this planning strategy. That other facet is the sales discovery process, and this entails dealing with the various parties involved in making the purchasing decision. Although this is discussed in greater detail in Chapter 5, there are a few points to be made now.

Procurement and Purchasing

In the typical sales process, a sales professional works with someone from the customer's procurement organization (to get the purchase order processed) and someone from their technical organization (to have their product or service evaluated and approved from a technical perspective). The procurement organization issues the purchase order as well as your payments. In general, purchase orders, or POs, are required for a customer to set aside funds to pay for the purchase of your products or services. A purchasing agent usually prepares the purchase order and negotiates the business terms of the relationship. By "business terms" I mean things like pricing, payment terms, contract volume, contract duration, warranties, post-sale training, and post-sale support.

Because the purchasing agent or procurement department plays a critical role in the sales process, most sales professionals know that they must work with these people as part of the sales process. Most sales professionals also realize that this is typically where the price pressure in a sales process originates. Purchasing agents are given a budgeted amount for the purchase of a product or service and are also given the price that has been negotiated up to this point. Their job is to negotiate whatever

additional discounts they can for the transaction, as well as negotiate the remaining business terms and conditions listed above.

Purchasing agents often have very little, if anything, to do
with the beginning of the sales process—the part when business
needs are discovered. Their role is at the end of the process. So,
when working with the procurement department, regard purchasing agents as you would any other part of the organization.
They should be included in the sales discovery process, in the
relationship-building process, and in the business solution that
you develop. The more you address the needs of the procurement department, the more likely they will support the purchase
of your products and services versus those of the competition.

Technical Review

Sales people must also work with the technical part of the organization. There is always someone to evaluate the technical merits of your solution. In the training business, this is the role of
the sales-training organization, the more general training organization, or possibly even the human resources department. If
you were selling technology, the customer's IT department
would be the ones to evaluate the merits of your solution.

When I say that the customer must evaluate the "merits of
your solution" from a technical perspective, what I mean is that
your product or service must work as specified in your proposal,
within the customer's existing technical environment. For example, a training program does not get delivered in a vacuum.
There were other training programs delivered before your training program is implemented and there will be additional training programs delivered after your training program is finished.
All of the training programs, yours included, must mesh for the
customer. Likewise, technology does not get purchased or work

in a vacuum. There is technology prior to the installation of your solution and there will be technology that will be installed afterwards.

So, you need to include the person or people in the technical organization—in the sales discovery process, in the relationship-building process, and in the business solution that you develop. Again, the more you address the needs of the technical evaluators, the more likely they will tend to support your solution versus that of the competition.

The Originating Executive

The person most sales people often forget to include in the sales process is the original executive who generated the need for your solution. Companies do not purchase training without an underlying business need. Companies purchase goods and services because they have a specific business need that must be addressed. This obvious point is often neglected during the sales process. Don't make that mistake.

You should see the originator as the most important person in the process. He or she is the source of the business need, likely the person funding the purchase, and often the final decision maker. I have seen many sales professionals lose a sale at the last minute owing to having ignored the source of the business need. Consistent with my other recommendations, the more you address the needs of the business executive at the source of the process, the more the individual will support your solution versus that of the competition.

One challenge to this admonition is addressing the stature of the executive within the organization. Many sales people feel intimidated when working with senior executives; however, the great equalizer in sales is the ability to help someone achieve his or her business objectives. For example, this past summer I was working with a client for which calling on senior executives was a real concern. The sales people on staff did not believe it appropriate to call outside of their technical contacts and they resisted my urgings to do so. However, there was one sales professional, very new to the business, who decided to give it a try.

I had also asked these sales people to stay abreast of the business issues facing their customers, and this sales person had read an article about his customer that allowed him to create a compelling value proposition. The customer was a major bank headquartered in the UK. The CEO at the bank had decided to make his bank the "direct bank of choice" in the UK. By "direct bank," the CEO meant that he wanted to be the most available bank in the UK and he would do this by giving customers two easy and immediate ways to access their funds—the Internet and a strong branch system.

The challenge faced by the CEO was that the branch system was heavily burdened by unnecessary costs. The strategy wasn't working because the CEO was unable to sufficiently lower the cost structure within the branch system to achieve his objectives. The sales person read the story and decided to contact the CEO. This CEO was a top business executive and the opportunity was both significant and intimidating for the new sales person. Nevertheless, he made the call, armed with an incredibly valuable proposition. He was welcomed with open arms by the CEO, and was able to follow through on the idea and make a considerable sale.

You cannot walk into a senior executive's office just for the purpose of presenting your wares—your ticket to the executive suite is a strong value proposition. Being armed thus so gives you the right to learn about the customer's business from the perspective of the executive office. While I can't guarantee that this approach will work every time, it is incumbent on all of us to make this effort part of our account plans.

The End Users

The end users of your products and services are no different from any of the other groups I have mentioned here. By understanding their perspective on the sales transaction, you can develop a more comprehensive and valuable solution.

Unfortunately, end users are often not included in the sales process because they typically *appear* to have the least influence over the final decision. What sales professionals often forget is that because this is the group that actually uses the business solution day in and day out, these folks can be a great source of new ideas. They may not be in on the decision to select your solution, but their input will help you shape a value-filled business solution.

The Triple Crown Winner

In this chapter, I provided the two high-impact account-planning tools and the third leg of the sales-planning "triple crown." The first tool was the account development cycle, a structured process for growing account relationships. The second tool was the sales process that facilitates a company's acquisition of goods and services. This second process was the driving factor that allowed you to move through the account development cycle.

An account plan details the means for working through the steps of the account development cycle and a strategy to optimize the sales process. It works in concert with the prospecting plan and the territory plan. Sales success does not happen by

accident. It is the direct result of the application of sound princi-
ples, such as those discussed in this chapter.

At the conclusion of both Chapter 3 and Part I of this book,
you now have sound concepts for each area of sales planning.
We move on to Part II of the book, where you will learn how
selling success in large part depends on sound sales execution.
As Woody Allen once said, "Ninety percent of success is just
showing up." And as Paul Goldner adds, "The remainder is
based on strong sales execution."

PART II

High-Performance Sales Execution

CHAPTER 4

Prospecting
Eliminating the Peaks and Valleys of Selling

Part I presented the basics of sales planning, encompassing the prospecting business plan, the territory plan, and the account plans. We are now in the part of the book that deals with sales execution, and in this chapter I provide a series of high-impact tips and techniques that will enhance your success in developing your new prospects. As the title of this chapter suggests, these are techniques that will help you avoid the peaks and valleys of sales that diminish your overall effectiveness in reaching your annual sales goals.

Stay Current!

In Chapter 3, I related the story of a sales professional who came across an article about the CEO of a large bank in the UK that could not achieve its business objectives. By tying the customer's business objectives to his solution, the sales professional won the account. Where did that seller come across the article? Google Alerts. This free service is an e-mail alert system that keeps you up to date on the latest Internet-posted items, based on search topics you specify. You can sign up for Google Alerts by typing "Google Alerts" into your search box and that will take you to the window where you can set up an account. I suggest that your topics list reflect the accounts on your territory plan (your top ten prospects and up to top ten accounts).

Google gives you a few choices as to how to receive your alerts, and I recommend doing them on a weekly basis. There are a few delivery options, but if you choose more frequently, you'll be receiving far more information than you can manage. Also, stick to requesting news, as opposed to some of the other research options, like video.

With your account set up as I have suggested, you will receive one e-mail per week for each of the accounts listed in your Google Alert profile. The e-mails will have a topic line and the first sentence or two about the article or news release. If the topic seems interesting, click it and read further. You can use the information in these articles to build your initial relationships with prospects, as well as enhance existing sales relationships.

Prioritize Your Prospects

When prospecting for new accounts, you should realize that not all prospects are created equal. There are always better prospects and there are always lesser prospects. So, you need to develop a methodology to prioritize those prospects, thereby making the best use of your time and efforts.

There are a number of ways to prioritize your prospects. Some of the more sophisticated approaches are discussed in my book *Red Hot Cold Call Selling* (AMACOM, 2006). However, at that level, you can always prioritize on the basis of size. Chapter

2 discussed how to determine company size, and you used that information to complete your territory plan. Now you can divide your accounts into three roughly equal sections, in descending order. If you have 100 accounts on your list, each section will contain approximately 33 accounts; if you have 300 accounts, each section will contain 100 accounts.

The top category of accounts (i.e., the largest accounts) become your A accounts, the middle category become your B accounts, and your third category becomes your C accounts. Just to clarify, your A accounts are your best ones, your C accounts are your third-best accounts. Remember, there are no bad accounts on your list because you already eliminated those when you drew up the territory plan.

Chapter 1 briefly mentioned subaccounts, or smaller accounts within a larger account. You should always select a manageable set of subaccounts to work with as well; it is better to do a good job with these subaccounts than a poor job with a larger number of accounts than you can manage.

The ABC Call Cadence

You want to prioritize your accounts so you spend more time with your A accounts and less time with your C accounts. The way to do this is by using what I call the "ABC call cadence." That is, you set call goals for each category of prospects, using the appropriate frequency for making those calls. Obviously, the more you call the accounts, the fewer accounts you can manage.

The ABC call cadence that seems to work best generally is:

A prospects	1 call per month
B prospects	1 call per quarter
C prospects	1 call per half-year

Typically, sales people who sell in a small and medium business (SMB) territory want to target a wider number of prospects than those selling to large accounts. If you are an SMB seller, your call cadence might be something like:

A prospects	1 call per quarter
B prospects	1 call per half-year
C prospects	1 call per year

On the other hand, sales people who sell in a large-account territory want to target deeper into a smaller set of accounts. For a large-account seller, your call cadence might be:

A prospects	1 call per month
B prospects	1 call per two months
C prospects	1 call per three months

As long as you are aware of the trade-offs you make, small accounts versus large accounts, you can develop an optimal ABC call cadence for your business.

You use the ABC call cadence because it takes time to develop personal relationships with your prospects. The first time that you call, the prospect will likely delete your message without listening to it. The next time you call, the prospect may listen to your message, then delete it. On your third call, the prospect may listen to your message and return the call, but not give you an appointment. And the fourth time you call, you may get the appointment but not do well. Finally, on your fifth call, you may develop an opportunity.

This is actually how it works in the real world. Be aware that it takes time to develop that relationship, and the ABC call cadence is the tool to ensure that you develop that relationship over time.

The Call Script

One of the most difficult concepts to teach new sales professionals is the need for a script when they pick up the phone to make a prospecting call. For some reason, scripting carries a negative connotation. Yet, to me, scripting is synonymous with preparation.

I often draw a comparison between professional sales and the Olympic Games. The Olympics represents athletics at the highest level, and that is what we should always strive for as professional sales people. To continue the analogy, there are three Olympic events in sales: making a new business prospecting call, holding a discovery sales meeting with your customer, and negotiating the close of the sale. Like an Olympic athlete who has prepared for many years for that Olympic event, you too must prepare for your sales events.

Making a prospecting call is not easy. I can tell you that from experience, and I can also tell you that by virtue of having observed clients try to make these calls during coaching sessions that we run. When you talk about the key elements of a prospecting script, every student in the class nods at the instructor, noting that they understand the concept and the rationale. Yet, when asked to make a real prospecting call, in the privacy of a closed office, even the most senior, seasoned sales professionals are often brought to their knees.

Many sales professionals know what to do, but the words just don't seem to come out of their mouths. In the rare instance that a seller can muster the courage to make a call, his or her words might come out like those in Figure 4.1.

FIGURE 4.1   **A General Prospecting Script**

> Hello, Bob.
>
> This is Paul Goldner of the Sales & Performance Group. I am the new account manager on your account and I wanted to come by your office to meet and introduce myself.
>
> Also, I wanted to make sure you are up to date on the new products and services we have recently brought to market.
>
> Please give me a call at XXX-XXX-XXXX.

The script in Figure 4.1 might not look all that bad—until you compare it to the script we propose you use, as shown in Figure 4.2.

I have stated unequivocally that there are better prospects

FIGURE 4.2   **Illustration of a Model Prospecting Script**

> Bob Jones, please. [pause]
>
> Hello Bob. This is Paul Goldner of the Sales & Performance Group. How are you today? [response]
>
> Great! One of the chief concerns we are hearing from others in your position is the need to improve sales and sales margins while minimizing the opportunity cost of taking sales people out of the field. Is this the same issue impacting your business or are there other more pressing concerns? [Mr. Jones responds.]
>
> Great! We have been very successful in helping companies like yours overcome issues very similar to these. What I would like to do is ask you a few more questions to better understand your needs and to help develop the best solution for you? Do you mind if I ask you these questions now?

and there are less impactful prospects. In a similar fashion, there are better prospecting scripts and less impactful prospecting scripts. Figure 4.2 has the key elements for having an impact and so the figure serves as a model script.

A Nice Greeting

The first major element is the question, "How are you today?" This is much more than a nice question. It gets the prospect to join in your call. This happens to be the question I use, but you can ask a similar question at this point. The key is to ask a question that gets the prospect to speak. Once the prospect responds, almost no matter what is said, your prospecting call becomes quite a bit warmer, owing simply to the fact that the prospect is now part of a two-way conversation.

As I mentioned, "How are you today?" is the question I have used successfully for many years. However, when I make this recommendation in my seminars, I often meet resistance from

FIGURE 4.3 A Prospecting Script for Telesales

Bob Jones, please. [pause]

Hello Bob. This is Paul Goldner of the Sales & Performance Group. How are you today? [response]

Great! One of the chief concerns we are hearing from others in your position is the need to improve sales and sales margins while minimizing the opportunity cost of taking sales people out of the field. Is this the same issue impacting your business or are there other more pressing concerns? [Mr. Jones responds.]

Great! We have been very successful in helping companies like yours overcome issues very similar to these. What I would like to do is ask you a few more questions to better understand your needs and to help develop the best solution for you. Do you mind if I ask you these questions now?

those who feel it is not professional enough. As a result, I offer an alternative: "Our records show that you are the Vice President of Sales at your company. I just wanted to confirm that this is your actual title." Using this question, you not only get the prospect to speak but confirm an important piece of information.

While I agree that the latter question allows you to achieve two objectives instead of one, I believe that the former fits better into the flow of a prospecting call. After all, the most important objective in making a prospecting call is to get to the sales discovery process going. Note, however, that if you do not begin with a trivial question, the remainder of your call will be difficult.

The Business Issue

The second major element in a prospecting script is the business issue. In Figure 4.2 (the model prospecting sample script), the business issue is presented as follows: "One of the chief concerns we are hearing from others in your position is the need to improve sales and sales margins while minimizing the opportunity cost of taking sales people out of the field." This is in stark contrast to stating that you are "the new account manager in the prospect's region and want to stop by the office to introduce yourself."

There are several major points here. First, when you tell the prospect that you want to have a meeting to introduce yourself, there is no value in that statement for the prospect. You are not giving the prospect a compelling reason to meet with you. On the other hand, by telling the prospect that "one of the chief concerns we are hearing from others in your position" implies that you have some valuable information for the prospect. Indeed, one of the most powerful tools you have as a sales professional is your familiarity with what others are doing in the market. The prospect clearly has a good view of what is going on in his or her own company, but cannot possibly have the same view of the market as does a sales professional. By sharing market trends with the prospect, you are adding value to the sales process.

Taking this one step further is the business issue itself. You are telling the potential customer that you can help them with a significant concern that has a high potential for impacting their business in a positive manner. Your ability to differentiate yourself during the sales process is very important. If you cannot differentiate yourself in a competitive market, you are likely doomed to compete on price alone. And competing on price is perhaps the worst basis because there is always someone who can provide the same product or service cheaper. So, by introducing a business concern early on in your script, you provide the prospect with a compelling reason to act, as well as differentiate yourself from other sellers in the market. Your competition probably is using the script in Figure 4.1, not the script in Figure 4.2!

Sometimes we have gone so far as to compare the effectiveness of a script like the one in Figure 4.1 to that of one in Figure 4.2. There is really no comparison. The Figure 4.2 script typically yields a 25 percent call-to-meeting ratio. Using a script like the one in Figure 4.1 diminishes the effectiveness of your completed call-to-meeting ratio to as little as 10 percent, possibly even lower. If you return to your prospecting business plan presented in Chapter 1, you will see the material impact this will have on your sales results.

The Open-Ended Follow-Up Question

The third major element in a good prospecting script is a larger, open-ended question that follows the business issue. The question that we recommend is, "Is this the same issue impacting your business or are there other more pressing concerns?" The exact wording is not significant here—it is the question itself that is important.

When you pose the business-issue question in your script, you cannot possibly know if this matter is relevant to the person you are calling. The best you can do is research your prospects and pose what you believe to be a valid question, given the current market environment. It should go without saying that the business issue should be something you can resolve with your company's product. If not, you will have little to sell at the end of the sales process. But because you cannot possibly know whether the business issue is relevant to this specific call, the follow-up question, "Is this the issue impacting your business or are there other more pressing concerns?" is extremely important.

First, this follow-up question gets the customer talking again. In sales, the customer should always do most of the talking. I like to recommend that 80 percent of the time with the customer, it is the customer who is doing the talking. You should be listening and taking notes. This leaves you 20 percent of the time to speak, and most of that time should be devoted to additional questions that encourage the customer to talk even more.

Second, it doesn't really matter how the prospect answers this question. If the prospect acknowledges that the business issue you posed is in fact a concern, you are well on your way to a sales discovery meeting. On the other hand, if the business issue is not a concern for the prospect, his or her answer will tell you what is of concern. Either way, you are well on your way to achieving your objective—a sales discovery meeting.

Closing the Prospecting Call

The fourth major element of your prospecting script is the close. When you are prospecting, the close is your getting to the sales discovery meeting. If you are in field sales, you do this by using the last two sentences in Figure 4.2. If you are in telesales, you can use the script in Figure 4.3.

* * *

In conclusion, the words you use in your script ought to be your own. The words that appear in these scripts are what I use and may not be appropriate for your product or situation, your culture, or your personality. To review, the major elements are:

1. Ask a trivial question at the start of your script to get the prospect speaking and be engaged in your conversation.

2. Pose a business issue of likely concern to judge the relevance of your approach.

3. Ask a clarifying, opened-ended question to either confirm the issue or discover alternative concerns.

4. Go for the close, which is to get to the sales discovery phase, either a face-to-face meeting or on the phone.

Monitor Your Progress

One of the best features of being a professional seller is that small, incremental improvements in your execution can result in significant increases in your results—and in your personal income. So, it makes a lot of sense to measure everything you do and compare it to industry norms so that you can judge how you are doing and make improvements where necessary.

As far as prospecting is concerned, the key ratios to measure are as follows:

❑ Completed calls to dials

❑ Meetings to completed calls

❑ Opportunities to meetings

I have studied these ratios over many years and Figure 4.4 presents my results. While these results may seem impressive, keep in mind that these are the results of sales professionals who have worked with us for relatively long periods of time (4 to 6 months per person). I am not sharing these results to brag about the success of our program but, rather, to allow you to benchmark your prospecting skills against those of high-performing sales professionals.

Keep in mind also that our client base is skewed to-

FIGURE 4.4 **Key Prospecting Ratio—Overall**

Ratios	Norm
Completed calls to dials	40%
Meetings to completed calls	49%
Opportunities to meetings	50%

ward larger, global corporations, though the results also reflect smaller, local corporations. Sellers in many large corporations have the advantage of working under the umbrella of a global brand, and global brand recognition can do nothing but help your prospecting efforts. If you work in a local corporation, without the benefit of a global brand, consider scaling the results down by 20 percent. These new results are presented in Figure 4.5.

To compare your results to those in either Figure 4.4 or Figure 4.5, track your results over a relatively long period of time. It can be misleading to compare your results for a single week to those provided here, for example. At the least, record your results for one entire quarter, if not longer, before making any comparisons. Using results for an entire quarter or longer you average away any unusual events that might have been temporary setbacks.

Remember that you compare your results to the benchmarks for remedial purposes. Underperformance in any of these areas

FIGURE 4.5 Key Prospecting Ratios for Non-Branded Companies

Ratios	Norm
Completed calls to dials	32%
Meetings to completed calls	39%
Opportunities to meetings	40%

has specific diagnoses and corrective paths. On the other hand, overperformance should lead you to understand that you are doing something special. If this is the case, try to understand what it is so you can replicate it and also share it with others in your company.

If your ratio of completed calls to dials is consistently less than 25 percent, there are two remedies. First, check the times that you are calling; they may not be prime prospecting times. In the United States, prime prospecting times are before work (i.e., before 9:00 AM), during lunch (i.e., 12:00–2:00 PM), and late afternoon extending into after work (i.e., 4:00–6:30 PM). However, best times vary by region and culture. In certain cultures, businesspeople take an extended lunch and often work much later into the evening. In other cultures, mornings start much later. To determine what prospecting times are best for your business, track the ratio of completed calls to dials by hour for several weeks. The hours with the highest ratio of completed calls to dials are prime times for you.

Types of Completed Calls

Relevant to this matter of prospecting ratios is the definition of a completed call. Completed calls can take place in two different ways. The first is when you call a prospect and the individual happens to pick up the phone (a "call out"). These calls most likely occur during prime calling times. The second is when you leave a message, and the message has such an impact that it motivates the prospect to call you back (a "call back"). To count these as completed calls, you must speak to the prospect when he or she calls you back. If they are motivated enough to leave you a message on voice mail, though, assume that you will eventually speak with the prospect in the near future and count this as a completed call as well.

The call back is the more likely result than the call out. The success of call outs directly relates to the quality of the message you leave. By quality, I mean the potential impact on the prospect's business of the issue you cite in your message. If the ratio of your completed calls to dials is less than 25 percent, consider reviewing your script.

The only significant difference between the script you use for leaving a voice-mail message and a completed call is that you omit the trivial, ice-breaking question at the beginning and make a few other minor changes to accommodate the fact that you are leaving a message and not speaking to the prospect. A voice-mail script based on Figure 4.2 is presented in Figure 4.6.

The Invitation to a Meeting

The second ratio in the prospecting benchmarks is that of meetings to completed calls. Figure 4.4 suggests that this should be 49 percent. Figure 4.5 suggests that this ratio should be 25 percent for less branded companies. If your results are less than expected, there are again two diagnostic procedures you can employ to improve your results.

FIGURE 4.6 **A Voice-Mail Prospecting Script**

Hello, Bob. This is Paul Goldner of the Sales & Performance Group. The reason I am calling is that we are seeing an interesting trend in the market. One of the chief concerns we are hearing from others in your position is the need to improve sales and sales margins while minimizing the opportunity cost of taking sales people out of the field. I was wondering if this is the same issue impacting your business or are there other more pressing concerns?

As you might imagine, we have been very successful in helping companies like yours overcome issues similar to these. I'm going to be in your area next Tuesday and would like to stop by and introduce myself. Please let me know if you are available at 3:00. I can be reached at XXX-XXX-XXXX.

This ratio reflects the quality of your customer interaction once the prospect starts talking to you. The first way to improve your results is to improve your basic script. Another way is to check your objection-handling skills. Since this topic is discussed in Chapter 6, let's defer the discussion on how to implement this improvement until then.

The Opportunity Realized

The final ratio in the benchmarking process is the relationship between your meetings and the opportunities for making a sale. Here, the big area for improvement resides in the sales discovery process, which is the focus of Chapter 5—so again, we wait to show how to improve in this crucial area.

Compelling Reasons to Persevere

In *Red Hot Cold Call Selling*, I talk about the concept of a company's five unique selling points and show how you can use them to build a strong prospecting strategy. The key point here is that if the first unique selling point doesn't work with the prospect, then you move on to the second unique selling point. In other words, if the first look you give the prospect doesn't work, change your look.

I want to reinforce the earlier point made in regard to scripts, for which I suggest using "business issues." Now, study Figure 4.7, which substitutes business issues for the unique selling points in the new-business development cycle. If the business issue you have posed in your first call does not work to get you the appointment, the recommendation is to move on to a new business issue for your second call to that prospect. If the first or

FIGURE 4.7 The New-Business Development Cycle

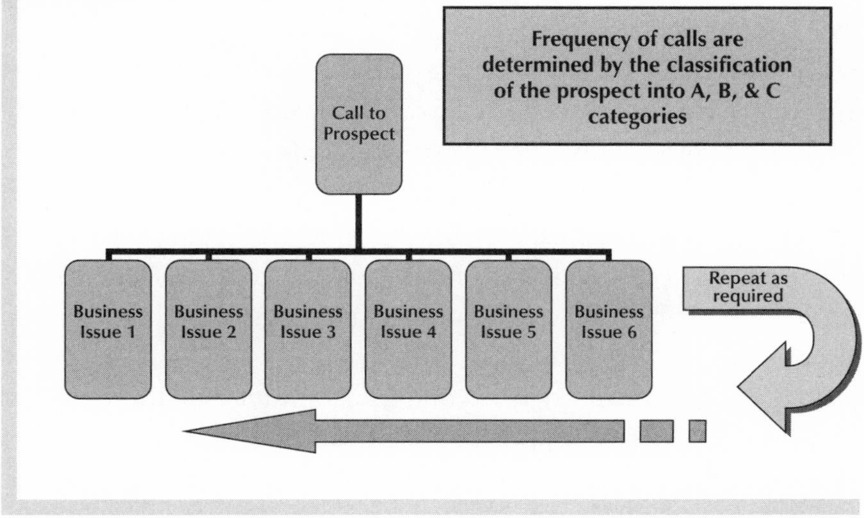

second business issues don't get you the appointment, the third business issue may. Don't give up on the prospect—keep trying.

Another key point to remember is that the new-business development cycle, or the prospecting process, does not end. If you reflect on the work you did setting up your territory plan, as discussed in Chapter 2, you selected certain accounts from all those in the market that you felt would maximize your sales results. Because you selected what you considered to be the best accounts, every account you selected was a good prospect. Remember, there are no weak accounts on your account list. This is true even if the prospect is classified as a B or C account. The B and C accounts are not as good as the A accounts, but they are far better than all of the accounts you did not select.

If you remove a prospect from your list because your calls are not being returned, this in and of itself does not make the prospect a bad one. You should continue to work with that prospect irrespective of your initial lack of success. It is up to you, as the sales professional, to find the compelling reason that will motivate the prospect to engage with you. If you get frustrated and remove the prospect from your list, you are only negatively impacting your ability to optimize your sales results.

Likewise, in Chapter 3, I recommended developing multiple contacts at each prospect. By having only one contact, you limit your initial success, but by having multiple contacts, you greatly improve your chances for a successful account penetration. In short, a large portion of your selling success will not be determined by the complexity of your sales strategy or the comprehensiveness of your approach. It will be impacted to the greatest extent by your determination to get out into the field or on the telephone, depending on whether you are a field seller or a teleseller.

*   *   *

This chapter provided some high-impact points about prospecting and new business development that will greatly improve your success rate. In Chapter 5, I discuss the sales discovery process, which is "the one thing that does it."

Sales Discovery
The One Thing That Does It

People are always surprised when I tell them that my mother was my sales mentor. I'm not sure when or where she started in sales, but the first time I saw her sell was when she was the lead sales person in my father's garment company. There she was, a working mother, outselling every man in the company. To make her achievements even more impressive, she took off at least 15 years from her career to raise a family.

After my father had passed away, she came to work for me in my computer training business. Although she had never touched a computer in her life, in a very short time she became one of the three top-performing sales people in our company (the same three salespeople, my mother included, who are mentioned in Chapter 2 regarding the large-account strategy). There she was in her early fifties, outperforming an entire nationwide company full of young men and women in their twenties and thirties, having never worked on a computer in her life. Many a year, she was the top sales person in the company and she never fell out of the top three once she made it there.

In the movie *City Slickers*, Billy Crystal, suffering from a mid-life crisis, goes on a trip out West to find himself. He struggles at every step because he is unfamiliar with the ways of the "Wild West." There is a cowboy named Curly along with him on the trip, played by Jack Palance. Curly had lived all his life in the Wild West. He was the expert! So Billy Crystal's character turned to Curly for guidance and leadership throughout the trip.

At a very poignant point in the movie, when Billy Crystal is really struggling, he turns to Curly, who is sitting on his horse, with the sun beaming down from above. Because of the low position of the sun in the sky, you can only see Curly's silhouette, not see his features. Before Billy Crystal can even ask his question, Curly anticipates the question and already has the answer. Curly holds his index finger in the air to indicate that there is only "one thing"—that it is up to each individual to discover the one thing that is the key to their life and their happiness.

At the end of her sales career, after my mother had been selling professionally for over 40 years, I felt like Billy Crystal looking up to Curly. I asked her what the most significant thing was that she learned in her career. Like Curly, she held up one finger; however, unlike Curly, she told me what that one thing was.

"The customer will always show you the roadmap to success."

The question then becomes, If the customer always shows you the roadmap to success, why is sales such a difficult profession to succeed in? She went on to tell me.

"The problem with most sales people is that they are always talking and not listening to what the customer is telling them. They are always trying to impress the customer with how good they are, how good their company is, and how good their products and services are." In other words, the key to selling success is in the sales discovery process, which is the subject of this chapter.

An Overview of the Discovery Process

The sales discovery process takes place after the successful completion of the prospecting process and is the heart of the overall sales process. The goal of the discovery process is to understand the customer's needs and, once they are understood, position your company for a sale.

Chapter 3, on account planning, described the account development cycle, the tool to guide you through the process of developing a large-account relationship. With it went a discussion of steps three through nine of the cycle. If you recall, we put the discussion of step 1 on hold. We now focus on that step: Identify the customer's needs. And the best way to do that is to ask good sales discovery questions.

The Necessity of Getting Beyond Yes or No

As a sales person, you can ask an open-ended question that requires a prospect to give you a detailed response, or you can pose a close-ended question that elicits little more than a grunt. Which do you think will get you to your sales quota?

Most people associate closed-ended questions with those that can be answered with a yes or a no. You certainly don't learn much about the customer if you pose simple yes or no questions. But closed-ended questions can be much broader than simple yes and no questions and still not yield the results you want. Instead, you want to learn to ask open-ended questions.

For some reason, when sales people are under pressure—
say, sitting in front of the customer—they "choke" mentally and
ask only closed-ended questions. If you have ever had a bad sales
discovery meeting with a customer, you can usually reflect on
the meeting later and analyze the questions you asked. Most
sales discovery meetings are unsuccessful because closed-ended
questions were asked far too early in the process. The way I remember this is: open-ended questions belong at the "opening"
of a sales discovery session; closed-ended questions belong at
the "close" of a sales discovery session. How's that for a mne-
monic?

A few days ago I gave the keynote speech at a national
sales meeting for a division of General Electric. GE is a world-
class company, one of the most successful out there. The company invests an incredible amount in developing their sales
people and so the sales force may be among the best trained
professionals in the world. At the end of the meeting, I talked
with the executive who had invited me. We had been good
friends for a long time. He is well schooled in the science
of professional selling, and he asked me to sit in on some
workshops.

At their national sales meeting, these professionals were
doing role-plays of the sales discovery process. Any guess what I
observed? Many of these sellers were asking closed-ended questions at the start of the sales discovery process. So, if asking
open-ended questions is a challenge even for GE's sales people,
it is obviously a universal problem. The good news is that there
is an easy way to fix this problem.

To overcome the significant challenge of framing open-
ended questions, I provide the Meeting Management Worksheet. I gave this worksheet to my friend at GE, and I am now
giving it to you, as Figure 5.1.

FIGURE 5.1 **Meeting Management Worksheet**

Your Objective:

1.	Identify the prospect's needs.
2.	Position your company.
3.	Gain your first small sale.
4.	Gain additional small sales.
5.	Gain your first large sale.
6.	Become the primary provider.
7.	Expand account penetration.
8.	Earn trusted adviser status.

Your Strategy:

Your Agenda:
- What are you doing now in the area of . . . ?

- Are there areas for improvement?

- What's your future direction?

- What's important to you in a relationship?

- Who else is involved in this decision-making process?

- Is there anything else I should know?

Your Unique Selling Points

1. USP I

2. USP II

3. USP III

4. USP IV

5. USP V

Your Next Step:

Preparation Is the Key

In Chapter 4, I told you that there were three Olympic events in sales: (1) picking up the phone and calling a prospect to get a face-to-face meeting, (2) having the face-to-face sales discovery meeting, and (3) negotiating the close of the sale. For all three, I have always advocated preparation. The event may last only ten seconds, but Olympic athletes prepare for their sport during the entire four years between Olympic Games.

I can't tell you how many times I have tried to make this point at meetings and conferences. I also can't tell you how many times I have stated it in my books and articles. Preparation is one of the core features of everything I do. This point never has the impact it should—until that GE national sales meeting.

In addition to having me as their keynote speaker, GE had what is known as an "up-close magician" to bring a little levity to the meeting. "Up-close" means that the magician wants the audience to sit as close as possible while he or she performs the tricks. It's as if the magician is challenging the audience to see the tricks behind the magic. The magician GE invited just happened to be the reigning "up-close" world champion. After completing his magic routine, he spoke about how he achieved world championship status.

The first time this magician went to the world championships, he aimed to compete—he wasn't expecting to win or even to make a top showing. Much to his surprise, however, he came in second. He also told us that he felt he was much better than the winner. He didn't go home to pout; rather, he went home to prepare to become the world champion next time. The next event was in three years.

A presentation at the world championships is exactly nine minutes long. If a contestant finishes even one second over the nine minutes, he is disqualified. If he finishes more than ten seconds before the nine minutes, he is also disqualified. Can you imagine making a sales presentation within a specified time limit, knowing that you had to make the sale or else abandon the attempt? Wow, what pressure!

Never mind the high caliber of the competition. The point of his talk that had the greatest impact, that got my attention and the attention of every sales person in the room, was that he prepared for three years—for a nine-minute presentation. If a person could prepare as he did for this world championship, how long do you think you should prepare for your world championships—what I have positioned as your three Olympic events?

Like the magician, we derive our livelihood from our Olympic events. But unlike magicians, we participate every day of the work week. That should make the argument for preparation even more compelling!

The Meeting Management Worksheet

You can use the Meeting Management Worksheet (Figure 5.1) to prepare like a world champion for this key segment of the sales process. Let's take a look at the worksheet from top to bottom, because it reflects the sales discovery process that I advocate as most effective.

Your Objective

The first section of your worksheet is titled "Your Objective," and this is where you write down your objective—your goals—for the sales meeting. Whenever you make a sales call, you should always have a business objective in mind. The days of the "Howdy! Call" where you just stop by with coffee and doughnuts are over. In today's competitive environment, most businesspeople don't have time for idle chitchat.

To the right of the "Your Objective" section are the steps of the account development cycle. Regardless of where you are in the cycle, your sales objective for the meeting should be to achieve the next step in the cycle. If this is the first time you are meeting with the prospect, your objective might be to get through step one—to gain an understanding of the prospect's needs. If this is the second time, your objective is to position your company relative to the prospect's needs. On your third meeting, your objective is to gain that first small sale.

Always understand where you are in the account development cycle with respect to each prospect you are going to meet. Ask yourself, "What have I achieved so far?" Use the account development cycle to link your meeting-management process to your account planning so as to ensure that you meet your objectives as fast as possible.

Your Strategy

The "Your Strategy" section of the worksheet calls for you to start thinking about how to position yourself for sales success. It's also a great place to begin differentiating your business solution in a competitive market.

Throughout the sales process, the prospect expects you to reinforce the strengths of your business solution and differentiate your company. In fact, that is one of your primary job responsibilities as a professional sales person. But because that prospect expects you to take a positive stance about your company, you gain little credibility by making this the centerpiece of your sales presentation. That is, when you say something positive about your business solution or your company, the prospect discounts your statements, many times by 100 percent, so you won't make much progress if you constantly boast about the company, the product, or yourself as a sales professional.

Instead, do something different—something everyone else in the market doesn't do, thereby catching the prospect or customer off guard. Rather than put the focus on you, your company, and your solution, bring something of value to your meeting.

When I speak of "value" I do not mean financial value. I mean business value, most often in the form of information. Through some of today's top search engines, such as Google or Yahoo!, it is easy to stay abreast of what is happening in your industry and with your clients as I suggested in Chapter 4. Use information you glean from Google Alerts that is relevant to your clients, your prospects, and your industry. Take that information to your meeting.

For example, before you start the meeting, you might say something like, "Did you see that article in the *Wall Street Journal* about. . . . ?" If the prospect says no, hand the individual a copy of the article. (Even if the prospect says that she saw the article, leave it behind anyway.) Then, use the article to make a relevant business point, positioning you and your company as informed and up to date—and implying that you might have more information down the road as well. Here's an example:

One of my clients sells to the financial services sector. At the start of the credit crisis of 2007/2008, there was an article about a bank in their customer set that was starting to wilt under the pressure. I sent my contact a copy of this article, asking him whether he thought the credit crisis was going to have a significant negative impact on his business.

Remember, this was at the start of the crisis, when companies like Citigroup, AIG, and Goldman Sachs had not revealed the extent of their losses. Imagine what this prospect was think-ing as the credit crisis began to grow. With the financial services companies shrinking or dissolving, it was almost certain that their purchases from companies such as my client would fall as well. Yet, in all likelihood my client's sales goals would grow; I'm sure he would have been intimidated if his sales goals had to remain merely what they had been in the past.

However, he received an e-mail from me, expressing an in-terest in his business. He started to wonder if that sales person (me) had a solution that might minimize the impact of the crisis on his business. Maybe, just maybe, he should pick up the phone and make the call. And so he does. I did have a solution to his problem.

Contrast this approach to the one most sales professionals choose. In fact, there is a great story that illustrates the path most often taken: A sales person walks into a purchasing agent's office and sees a large fish on the wall. He stands back, admires the fish, and then turns to the purchasing agent and says, "You must be a great fisherman." The purchasing agent replies by telling the sales person that he does not fish at all. He just wanted to put the fish there to see how many sales people would try to gain his favor by remarking about his fishing prowess.

Which sales person do you want to be—the one who earns the sale by bringing new, critical information to your clients, or the one who struggles to make a living talking about the fish on the wall? Do you want to be the consultative seller who catches the big fish by adding value to the customer's business, or do you want to be the small fish that's tossed back as undersized? Do you want to stand out from the rest of the sellers?

Your Meeting Agenda

The next part of the worksheet is the heart of the sales process— sales discovery. Remember my mother, who held up her index finger and said, "The customer will always provide you with the roadmap to success"? The agenda portion of the worksheet is where you build the framework to produce that roadmap. Basically, you ask a series of six types of questions.

The Background Question. To begin, you need to establish a baseline for the remainder of the meeting. The background question asks the prospect what the company is doing now in the area of . . . , which presumably is the area in which your product or service falls. For instance, let us assume that you are an energy consultant selling companies a means by which they can review their current energy efficiency. Your background question might be: "Can you tell me about the energy efficiency initiatives in your company now?"

The prospect's response to this background question provides the information you need to understand how your solution relates to the company's current situation. If the prospect is somewhat less than forthcoming, you can always ask secondary probing questions, like the following:

- ❑ Can you tell me more about that, please?
- ❑ Can you help me understand that better, please?
- ❑ Can you give me an example?
- ❑ Why do you do it that way?

Remember, you only go to one "first" meeting with a prospect. That means that, in your later meetings, you will need to adjust your beginning questions. For the first meeting, say, you ask about the energy efficiency initiatives now being implemented. Six months from now, when you have not spoken to the prospect, you need only update your understanding of the customer's baseline—say, by asking, "The last time we met, you told me about Initiatives *X, Y,* and *Z.* Can you tell me how you have progressed with these initiatives and what other changes I should be aware of, such as new initiatives, completed initiatives, or dropped initiatives?"

The Value Discovery Questions. You cannot do a good job of sales discovery without asking some value discovery questions. These are questions that probe the possibilities for change and supplementation. For example, "Given what you are doing now [based on the answer to your background question], are there areas for improvement?" A second value discovery question is, "Given what you are doing now, do you see any significant changes over the next six to twenty-four months?" (obviously inserting a relevant time frame for your industry).

The reason these two questions are critical is that there are only two ways to penetrate a new account with a standard product. By a standard product, I mean a product that is at the mature end of the product life cycle, a product for which there are a number of readily available alternatives, or a product that the customer tends to view as a commodity. The first way is to lower your price until your offer becomes so attractive that the customer has to switch from the competition to you. Of course, as mentioned earlier, after you make the first sale you are going to have to live with that pricing for a very long time.

The better way to penetrate an account is to give the prospect something he needs that he doesn't already have. Let me give you the example of a sales person selling mushrooms to supermarkets: When you sell a product to a supermarket, it is usually stacked on wooden palettes for easy movement around the warehouse. If you were selling cans of tomato paste, you might put 12 to 16 cans into a box. The boxes of tomato paste would then be stacked on a palette, so that the supermarket could easily move many palettes and hence a lot of tomato paste at one time.

When goods are received at the supermarket's warehouse, they are stacked palette on top of palette so that space is used efficiently and also so that the goods can be moved easily from place to place in the warehouse. Now, mushrooms are hardly a unique item, and I am sure that there are many mushroom growers for a supermarket chain to select from. However, one mushroom sales person took the initiative to go to his customer's warehouse to observe how inbound shipments of mushrooms were received, processed, and stacked. What he found was quite interesting.

He learned that mushrooms were costly to receive because they could not be stacked on palettes like other products. Rather, they required additional processing and handling because they crush and get bruised easily if other items are placed on top of them. His idea was to provide crush-proof packaging.

From the customer's perspective, the quality of a product is usually "good enough"—that is, if there are three manufacturers of a given item in the market, customers perceive all three versions as good enough for their purposes. This means that they have commoditized the product, service, or solution, and when a product, service, or solution is commoditized, the price becomes the major determining factor in the sale.

For you to challenge this direction, you must find things that the customer needs that he or she doesn't already have, such as the crush-proof packaging in this example. By adding a new feature to your product or service, you create a better solution and move it out of the commodity position. The value discovery questions help you do just that.

Asking the value discovery questions may open up the possibility of finding something the prospect needs. A positive answer to either of these questions usually gives you that opening. By bundling this additional value to your core product, you differentiate your solution in a competitive market and start to penetrate the prospect on the basis of value, not price.

An important point here is that the potential customer may not know what he or she needs, and the prospect's answers don't point to that need. So the other way to gain information on your prospect is to see how he uses your product or service in his business. In our example, the mushroom sales person went to the warehouse to understand the business better than the competition did and possibly better even than the prospect.

Of course, the needs that you uncover should be value that you can provide. Once identified, they are the means to differentiate your solution in a competitive market, compete on other than price, and penetrate new accounts without dropping your price tremendously to get that first order.

There is one other important point. Your prospect could tell your competitor about that great idea you bundled with your core product or service. Then, the competitor could copy your idea and provide it to the customer at a lower price. So, you never want to submit a proposal with only one value point or one point of differentiation. If you do, you place yourself and your proposal in a risky situation. Rather, provide a comprehensive solution with many great value points or ideas. The more value you put into your solution, the less possible it is for the competition to copy your solution and/or to provide it at a lower price.

The Value Management Questions. Your next question is, "What's important to you in a relationship with a company like ours?" To understand this question type, I need first to present a little background.

This is one of my favorite questions, for two reasons: (1) If a prospect has never purchased your product or service or one from your competition, he or she will spend at least some time learning about that product, service, or solution. If the prospect takes that time to learn about what you are selling, he or she will have preconceived notions about what is important in a relationship with the supplying company. (2) If the prospect has been purchasing your product type for many years, he or she will not only have preconceived notions about what's important in the relationship but also these notions will be hardwired into their procurement DNA. If you face either of these situations, you will see that the prospect always comes to the meeting with perceptions of what's important in a sales relationship. Recognize, therefore, that at this point, your solution may or may not align with what the prospect is looking for. If it does, you will probably win the sale; if it does not, and you do nothing to change those perceptions, you will probably lose the sale.

However, even if you lose the current sale, this does not mean that you can never sell to this company again. You will need to work with prospects over an extended period to understand their needs, find needs that they recognize, and help them understand what is truly important in a relationship with your company. Over time, you can remold the way a prospect views your product category; that is why you ask this question.

Likewise, if you don't know where the prospect is in terms of what is valued and what isn't, you cannot show that prospect how your value proposition is superior to those of the competition. Again, to eventually win the prospect, you have to work over time to remold the company's vision of what is important in a sales relationship. The starting point for this molding and remolding process is the value management question.

In the buying process, the prospect or customer usually

starts with a wide array of potential solutions and then fairly rapidly focuses in on two or three competing vendors. Let's call these few competing vendors the finalists. I am old-fashioned, but I like to believe that customers select the product or service that best fits what they perceive their needs to be. So, the sales process comes down to one point: Does your product or service best map the customer's needs? Keep in mind that a customer's needs include price, total cost of ownership, quality, delivery, post-implementation support, and other factors that are usually involved in the purchase of a product or service.

You need to ask the value management question to gain an understanding of your customer's value system. Does the company rank price highest or is preference given to total cost of ownership? Does the company assume that quality is a given, as they wouldn't be talking to you if you weren't a quality provider? Or do they want you to show them the more important features of your product or service? Are they interested in other basic features of the transaction, such as payment terms, length of agreement, volume associated with the agreement, and delivery schedules?

When you ask the question, "What's important to you in a relationship with a company like ours?" you ought to get a list of factors that might be important, such as price, quality, delivery, total cost of ownership, and reliability. There should be three to five items; if it is longer than that, you may want to help prospects understand the decision-making process a bit better. That is, they cannot possibly do an effective job of evaluating the selection points in the sale—at some point, they must refine their selection process to a few crucial areas.

Note that the list of concerns you are given is not necessarily in order of importance—that's because you have not asked the prospect to do so. Therefore, the value management question comes with a related probing question: "Can you help me prioritize these?"

Now let's see how a prospect might prioritize these points:

1. Price

2. Reliability

3. Delivery

4. Quality

5. Total Cost of Ownership

As you can see, the prospect has placed price at the top of the list. This tells you that he believes your product is a commodity and that there is little you can do during the sales process to change that. In the short term, that is true. Your most effective sales strategy in the short term is price and, as I've said, that can cause problems down the line.

Remember, you can enter the sales cycle in one of three places. The first place is early in the process. If you enter the sales cycle early, you will have the most time to mold and manage customer perceptions about what is important in a relationship with your company. If you enter the current sales cycle in the middle, you will have some chance to mold the decision-making process, but so will your competition. In fact, they may have entered the sales cycle earlier than you and that may limit your possibilities. Finally, you can enter the sales cycle on the late side. At the point of sale, or close to the point of sale, your ability to impact the decision-making process is limited. If your solution happens to align with the prospect's decision-making process, you are in good shape, however.

If your solution does not align with the customer's decision-making process, there is little that you can do to change that situation. Your only potential option is to lower your price, and lowering your price assumes that the prospect is looking for a low price. In fact, that prospect may not be looking for you to lower your price, in which case your options are even more limited.

I believe that lowering your price to win business sets a pricing precedent that will be hard to change as your relationship with a customer evolves. I also believe that the best sales strategy, bar none, is to have a full pipeline. A full pipeline allows you to walk away from a transaction that may not be good for you and your company in the short term.

The last thing to remember about value management is that sales is a process, not an event. Customers usually buy on a recurring basis. That means that they may go to market once a year, once every six months, once a quarter, once a month, or possibly some other interval. Whatever the procurement procedure is, there is usually an interval. While some industries tend to make single purchases (such as for life insurance, expensive medical equipment for doctors' offices, etc.), most follow the recurring pattern (such as software sales, computer sales, sales training, accounting and auditing services, etc.).

For customers that buy on a recurring basis, you can use this fact to significant advantage. Your sales cycle is automatically converted to an ongoing, never-ending process, so you should always be thinking about what you can do to mold your customers' perceptions of what is important in a relationship with your company.

Remember that where you enter the first sales cycle is more likely a function of good luck than anything else, but that you have control over the second sales cycle, third sales cycle, and so on. Even if you didn't enter the first sales cycle in the earlier stages, you can enter the sales cycle early in every sales cycle thereafter. Over the long run, you will have the opportunity to manage a customer's perceptions of what's important in a relationship. How you manage those perceptions, and to what extent, is up to you.

To begin, make certain that your contacts are on your company's mailing list so that they get all of your company's press releases. Set up Google Alerts or some other news-tracking service for your significant customers and important prospects. Also read industry journals—not only journals about your own industry but also journals about your customers' industries. You need to understand their view of the world. In sales, the more you know, the better you will do. You use the information you gather to help manage those customer perceptions about what's important in a relationship.

When you win a sale and you become either the incumbent provider or the majority provider, you will have until the next purchasing point to find additional value or points that are unique to your company or product in the market. You also have that interval to manage those customer perceptions. These are not trivial points.

Also, as the incumbent provider, you have access to greater customer information and you have direct access to that customer. Let me repeat, it is your account to lose. If you are doing your job properly and meet with the customer over time, continue to evaluate their needs and understand their business applications, and continue to strengthen your relationship not only on a personal but also a business basis, it's hard to imagine how you could lose the account.

However, sometimes sales people forget what made them successful. For instance, many sales professionals wait a year to reconnect with their customers. They spend no time under-

standing how their product or service was applied and no time
observing how the customer's needs may have evolved. If you
let this happen, you will have done little, or possibly nothing, to
manage your account. When it comes time for the next purchasing decision, you'll find yourself on the outside looking in.

The Decision-Maker Question. The next decision-maker question
is: "Who else is involved in the decision-making process?" This
question has its roots in the approach described by Robert B.
Miller and Stephen E. Heiman in their groundbreaking book
Strategic Selling (Grand Central Publishing, 1988).

What you are trying to discover with this question is the buying influences in the sales process. Note that I say "buying influences" and not people. A buying influence can be a person,
but it is usually not. For example, when you are selling to
smaller companies or even to family units, you can often find
one person playing the role of two or more buying influences.
On the other hand, when you are selling to large corporations,
buying influences are represented by multiple people, such as
when a company has two divisions each headed by an individual.
In general, there are two types of buying influences.

❏ *The usual buying influences.* If you study the sales process
in just about any industry and just about anywhere in the world,
you will find that the salesperson usually works with (1) the customer's purchasing influence and (2) the customer's technical
influence. The customer's purchasing influence is represented
by a person or group of people who facilitate the acquisition of
goods and services. They are typically found in the customer's
purchasing or procurement area, and they get involved later in
the sales process, sometimes after the client has selected the
provider. The purchasing influence usually brings a strong price

focus to the transaction and/or relationship, and generally acts in the best interests of their company and not in a win/win mode.

It is rare even for purchasing agents to focus on price alone. You bring other elements to the sales relationship so you have the ability to negotiate on behalf of your company and create a win/win outcome for both parties. If the purchasing influence does focus primarily on price, ask, "Is price your only concern?" This usually brings out other potential issues, such as payment terms, length of agreement, warranty terms, and volume that are covered by the agreement. Ask yourself: who is going to answer yes to the question of price being their only concern? A positive answer implies that delivery is irrelevant, as would be a product or service that does not perform as specified. Better, then, to make the other purchasing concerns obvious so that you can create an effective, win/win outcome.

The second usual influence in any sales process is the technical one. This entails a technical evaluation of the product or service required prior to purchase. The purchasing company wants to ensure that your product or service is consistent with, work with, integrate into, or use as much of present company assets as possible.

The technical influence is also looking at the technical features of your product, and they are likely to produce a checklist of features to look for in a solution. The only question here is, whose checklist will they be using—their own, yours, or the competition's? The answer to this question is the very reason it is so important to build a relationship with the technical influence as early in the sales cycle as possible. Obviously, the best position is to have the customer or prospect reading from your checklist. The earlier you enter the sales cycle, the easier that is to accomplish and the longer you have to manage their perceptions. Thus, the value management process and the early engagement apply to all decision makers, to the customer organization, and to the technical decision maker specifically.

❑ *The unusual buying influences.* In addition to the usual buying influences, there are the unusual buying influences. By unusual we mean the two buying influences that are typically not included in the sales process. The economic influence and the end user influence are the two influences often neglected in the sales process. By including these buying influences in your sales process, you can gain a competitive edge over your competition because you will be doing something different, which is of incremental value to you as a professional sales person.

In many ways, the economic influence is the most important of all the buying influences because it typically confirms the sale—the true decision maker. The economic influence is usually also the source of the business problem that necessitates the purchase of a solution. However, you have to be careful to not let the economic influence gain too much relative importance.

For my sales business, training is typically purchased by either the procurement department or the training department of a company. However, I always ask myself why they are buying the sales training. Is it for their own needs or the needs of others in the organization? The same is true for a technology purchase. It can be made based on the technical influence or the purchasing influence, but more often than not it is on behalf of someone else in the organization. This is important to know because, if you don't understand why a purchase is being made and where the request is coming from, it will be hard to truly understand the customer's needs and then add value to the purchase.

Figure 5.2 shows how a typical customer requirement comes into existence. At the start of a customer requirement (i.e., a purchase), you see a business process owner (BPO). The BPO is

FIGURE 5.2 How a Purchase Comes to Be

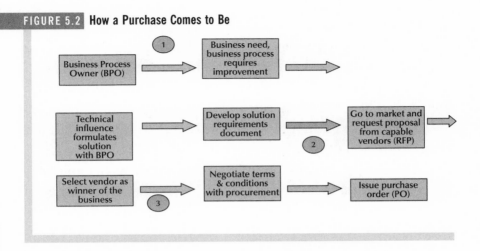

often the economic influence. The BPO observes a business process in action, sees where it is optimized and where it is not, and may, on the basis of a less than optimal process or outcome, desire to change the process. It is this desire for change that generates the need for a product, service, or, much more appropriately, a solution. This completes step 1 of the procurement process.

The BPO then goes to the internal technical influence, as the BPO or economic influence would not typically know the capable vendors. By "capable vendors" I mean vendors that could actually help. I would doubt that business vice presidents are well versed in the sales-training vendors in the market. I would also doubt that they are well versed in the technology vendors, even though many of these companies are household names like Microsoft or IBM. The BPO explains the business challenge and then develops, in partnership, an appropriate solution. The technical influence then prepares a requirements document and goes to the market to fulfill the requirement—using a request for proposal, or an RFP. This is step 2 of the procurement process (see Figure 5.2). At this point in the process, much of the value in the solution has already been extracted by the customer. Because the customer has developed the solution without your help (but possibly with the help of your competitor), the product has become a mere commodity. This means that, in most cases, there's very little value you can add from the customer's perspective, and they are simply looking for a part or item to fill their need. At this point, you have completed step 2 in the process.

If one of your competitors has participated in the solution-creation process, that competitor will be in a secure position. If you find yourself outside this process, it is difficult to compete on value and, as indicated earlier, price may be your only sales option. On the other hand, there is no reason you cannot be the company that has extracted that value by being the first one to reach the economic influence and participate in the solution-creation process, ready to win the role of supplier. Once you are at this point, you are entering step 3 of the procurement process where the final vendor selection is made, and the terms and conditions of the contract are negotiated.

Let's assume that you are one of several vendors bidding for the right to supply the item and fill the customer's need for a solution. The sale will be highly price-focused at this stage. By asking your decision-maker question, "Who else is involved in the decision-making process?" you can assess all the influences and their needs.

As a general rule of thumb, I assign a value of 25 percent to each of the four buying influences, even if it is easy to argue that the economic influence is the most important. For example, if I have met with each of the four influences, I give myself a high chance of winning the business (25% × 4 buying influences = 100% chance). If I know three of the four buying influences, I give myself a 75 percent chance of winning the business—and so on.

You can avoid the competitive bidding process altogether, or at least have it heavily weighted in your favor, by starting your sales cycle at the beginning of the procurement process, as opposed to waiting for an RFP to be issued. The downside is that you may run into some internal political turbulence by bypassing the usual procurement process. You also may have sidestepped the need for an independent technical evaluation, which may bother the technical influence. This is something that you have to evaluate on a case-by-case basis.

If you do start your sales cycle at point 1 in Figure 5.2, there may be one other step that you need to consider, and this is addressed in Figure 5.3. Figure 5.3 is actually an interim figure that will show you how we get from Figure 5.2 to Figure 5.4. In Figure 5.3, we introduce the fourth buying influence. It is called the End User buying influence.

Because end users are well versed in the existing business process, they are best positioned to help you understand how

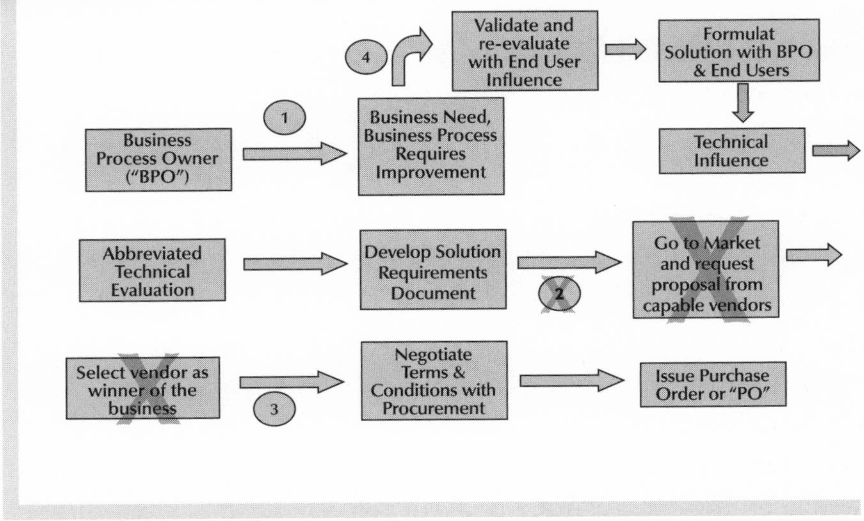

FIGURE 5.3 Interim Procurement Process Driven by Sales Professional

the current process is not meeting the company's needs. They can tell you what good ideas, or value points, to include in your proposed solution and what may not be good to include. Indeed, end users, whether they be factory workers or programmers, truck drivers or sales executives, can be great sources of information. Remember also that your competition is not likely to include either the end user or the economic influence in their sales processes. They are probably being reactive, waiting until the customer brings an RFP to the market instead of helping to identify the need at its source.

So, by soliciting the information from end users, you can help shape the BPO's needs assessment, making a valuable contribution that the company may view as a time and cost saver. The BPO can then quickly formulate a solution, submitting it for an abbreviated technical evaluation, and develop the purchasing documents that incorporate your input. It's likely, then, that the bidding process will be shortened or even eliminated, and that the BPO will move directly to negotiating the terms and conditions of the relationship with you. Once the terms and conditions are set, the customer can then issue the purchase order. The proper procurement process driven by the sales professional is shown in Figure 5.4.

The Concluding Question. Your last question needs to be: "Is there anything else I need to know to make this solution or proposal as meaningful as possible for you?" With this question you make sure that you have done everything possible to gather the information you require.

Your Unique Selling Points

You'll notice, in Figure 5.1, the section alongside "Your Agenda" has been headed as "Your Unique Selling Points." These unique

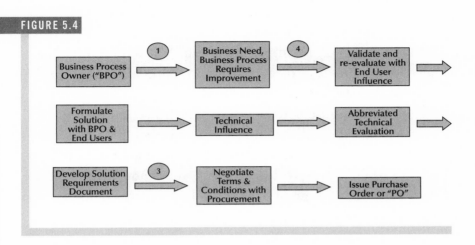

FIGURE 5.4

selling points represent your company's five greatest strengths in the market. Each should answer the question, "Why should I do business with your company?" These strengths differentiate your company in a competitive market and also are five significant, potential value points a customer could receive as part of a relationship with your company. By "value points," I mean that each point conveys one significant value proposition to the customer. Because old selling lore tells us that most sales take place after the fifth call, we have always recommended that you maintain a list of your company's five greatest strengths in the market.

The idea of this section of the worksheet is to ask your questions and discover the customer's needs. Just opposite of your questions and your notes containing the customer's needs (yes, you can take notes in a sales meeting, and you can use your worksheet for this purpose), you have your Unique Selling Points. The worksheet confirms it: you are the bridge between the customer's needs and your company's unique selling points—its five greatest value propositions. The customers cautiously walk across the bridge as you coach them, reinforcing the sale and supporting its implementation. You have helped them relieve their sources of discomfort by creating a successful solution for the customer.

The next time those customers sense discomfort, they will remember your business solution and invite you for a new evaluation and proposal. They will not be as cautious the next time, either, as they will have learned that you know what you are doing, that you build great bridges to their success, and that you stand behind what you say.

Your Next Step

As they say, Rome was not built in a day. It takes time to understand the customer's needs and to build your solution. There is often more than one meeting on the road to success, and you need a way to link one meeting to the next. That is what the "Your Next Step" section of the worksheet is designed to help you do. Here, you list the actions you will take to follow up on this meeting.

* * *

The sales discovery process is at the heart of the sales process. Following the process may be the most important thing you do as a professional sales person. The chapter used the metaphor of the Olympic Games to demonstrate the importance of asking the best questions. It used the bridge metaphor to show the role of the sales professional in meeting customer needs with company or product solutions. Let us now move to the next chapter, where you will learn how to handle customers' objections to your products and services. Yes, this method is unique, effective, and easy to implement, so why not give it a try?

CHAPTER 6

Handling Objections
The Easy Way!

If I were writing this book the old-fashioned way, I would tell you not to worry about objections. I could say that objections are simply the customers' requests for more information or that objections are good because they indicate interest. I could teach you popular objection-handling techniques such as "Feel—Felt—Found" or my favorite, "Present an Alternative."

If you are not familiar with these techniques, let me show you what they are. Assume that the customer told you your price is too high. You respond with the "Feel—Felt—Found" technique: "I can understand how you *feel*. Many of my best customers also have *felt* that way. However, when they gave me a moment to explain, they readily *found* that they received the lowest total cost of ownership. For example, we were recently able to help a local insurance agency to save $20,000 in labor costs by implementing our new technology."

The "Present an Alternative" is my favorite technique. You respond: "That's one way to look at the situation. However, another way to look at it is [here comes your alternative] if you consider the potential impact of our new technology on your business, you would see that you would receive a much greater *value* with our solution. For example, we were recently able to help a local insurance agency grow sales by $20,000 after implementing our new technology."

I could continue with this approach by providing examples of the other two commonly used objection-handling techniques I am aware of, "Ask an Open-Ended Question" and "Ask a Leading Question." However, before I do that, there are some much more important things to understand.

There Are a Limited Number of Objections

Whenever I teach a seminar on the topic of handling objections, I wind up asking the question, "How many objections do you think there are in the world?" The answers I get are always humorous, though I don't dare laugh at the time. One response is that the number of objections is approximately the same as the number of grains of sand on a beach. A more existential one is that there are many, but one cannot calculate how many because there is no way to be sure that you have them all. And the cultural response is that it depends on the location of the seller— different for, say, the United States, Russia, China, or Africa.

Yes, there are some differences between selling in the United States and in Africa, but regional differences are usually fine details, not major factors that impact your sales success. For example, when I make a prospecting call in my home market, southern New York State, just 50 miles north of New York City, I use a prospecting script in which I say something like,

"Bob Jones, please.

Bob responds, "This is Bob."

"Hi, Bob. This is Paul Goldner, of the Sales & Performance Group. *How are you today?*"

Now, in Europe, it is inappropriate to ask a question along the lines of "How are you today?" if you don't know the person you are speaking with. I remember the first time I used that question in a prospecting script in Europe; I was nearly expelled from the country. This was considered a significant error on my part, and I learned very quickly not to do it again.

In my book *Red Hot Cold Call Selling*, and in my prospecting seminars based on the book, I stress the importance of asking that question. With a prospecting call, I have just identified the person I am looking for as Bob Jones. Then I introduce myself. If I were to continue to the next section of the script, without engaging the person at the other end, I would be making a significant error. I would be talking *at* the person instead of *with* the person.

When I teach this program in the United States, I leave my question as "How are you today?" For the most part, no one in this country takes this as an intrusion. However, when I teach the program in Europe, I change the question. I cannot forgo using a question, because I already know that the call won't work without some way to engage the listener. So what do I do?

I ask a question that will work, such as, "I understand that you are the CFO at your company. Is that true?" At this point, I engage the person, make contact, and begin to communicate. The cultural element in sales does exist and it is important to take it into consideration. Yes, you do make minor changes to your sales process in different locations and cultures. However, these changes are minor. Just be sure the question is culturally appropriate.

The Right Model for Handling Objections

If truth be told, there are only four objections—in all of professional sales! These objections are price, competition, "will it work," and "not now." That is it. There are no more, no matter how far and wide you look. So why are objections such a dreaded part of the sales process? The answer is that each objection can come in many different forms.

So, my model for handling objections identifies the four basic objections that emerge in all sales attempts. The model tells us that there are many ways each objection can be stated, so we must become adept at recognizing each type and understanding exactly what the customer has just said.

The Price Objection

The key words for the price objection are "lower or lowest total cost of ownership" and/or "value." These key words or key phrases must be in your response to the price objection for you to have a world-class response. Need I say more? So, let's move on to the second of the four types of objections.

The Competition Objection

When you make a prospecting call to a potential customer, the prospect might say that he or she "works with XYZ Company." That prospect could just easily have said that he or she does that task personally. "Doing it myself" is actually a form of the competition objection. It is called the "internal competition objection," since the prospect, in essence, is your competition.

Let's say that you have just graduated from college, you live in a fair climate year-round, you like working outdoors, and you like being your own boss. Let's also assume that you studied horticulture in college. Upon graduation, you decide to open your own lawn-mowing service. You start selling your service by going door to door. At the first door, the prospect turns you down, saying, "I'm sorry, but we already work with Jim's Lawn Care. We have been with him for so long it would be unfair of us to change at this point."

You are discouraged, but you are not willing to give up yet. You go to the next door, and this time you hear: "I used to use Jim, but with the downturn in the economy, I do that myself now. I'm sorry, but thanks for stopping by."

What happened here from an objection perspective? The first thing you should note is that you didn't get very far because you received the competition objection. What does the competition objection tell you? It tells you that the customer is already set with respect to procuring your products or service. In the first case, the prospect was happy with his present service; in the second case, the prospect doesn't hire anyone from the outside to do this work. There is really no difference between Jim and the "do it yourself" guy.

And therein is the key to objection handling: though there are only four types of objections, there are more versions of each type than you can imagine. And that's where the seller often gets into trouble. Instead of recognizing that these variations are the same type of objection, he tries to reinvent the wheel by creating specific responses to each variation.

Consider one way to handle the competition objection. Suppose, instead, you responded to the first prospect like this:

"That's okay. Jim's Lawn Mowing and Maintenance is a very good company, and I'm sure they do a great job for you. However, we have found that we can often be a great *supplement* to some of the things that Jim offers. For example, one of the things we pride ourselves on is our tree service. Most lawn mowing companies do not offer this second service. By offering both services, you have a single point of contact for both your land and tree needs."

Alternatively, you could use the account development cycle, and position yourself for the tree work. This would be your first small sale at the accoount. Over time, you can build your track record of success, and ultimately take over the lawn business as well.

The competition objection is, in my opinion, the most difficult of the four objection types to handle. As you can see, negative statements are not advised. Even a statement such as, "Let me tell you why we are a much better company than Jim's for this type of work" will cause you a lot of harm. Likely, the person you are speaking with made the decision to select Jim's service. Anything you say negative about Jim also negatively reflects on that person. Any statement that implies the prospect may have made the wrong decision will only make the prospect defensive.

That is why this is a difficult objection to counter. If you are not careful, you can damage what little relationship you have with that person. Using words like *supplement, complement,* or *in addition to* allows you to sidestep the direct comparison of your company and the competition. The metaphor I use to keep me doing the right thing in these situations is that of a charging bull, its horns pointing straight at you, getting ready to gore you in the stomach unless you step out of the way. However, like a skilled matador from Mexico, you step out of the way just at the right moment. Unlike the matador, sales professionals do not have red capes. Rather, our tool of choice is the words that we use at the right moment to build a good relationship with our prospects.

Now let's consider how to respond to the "do it yourselfer." Here's a suitable reply:

"That's okay. I'm sure that you do a great job in this area. However, what we have found is that we can often be an effective supplement to some of the things that you do yourself. For example, one of the things that we pride ourselves in is our certified fertilizer service. Most people who mow their own lawn are not certified to handle the chemicals required to do proper lawn maintenance through the seasons. We are, and we apply the proper chemicals to your lawn at the right times throughout the year."

If you compare the responses, you see that they are almost identical. The exact wording is of little consequence; what is of consequence is that you identify the competition objection as such when you hear it, and that you avoid directly confronting the objection, thus damaging your relationship with the prospect or customer.

Reference Examples, Both Actual and Synthesized

These examples bring to mind another important point. You should always have a reference story or two that show exactly how you can do the "supplemental" activity. Assuming you have other clients, you can refer to them to illustrate your point and make the potential customer feel comfortable about giving you at least a portion of the business. Note: If you do not have good reference stories to illustrate your point, "synthesize" a story to illustrate your point—that is, combine two or even three references that serve together to demonstrate the points you are making.

To illustrate how to synthesize a reference story, let me assume that you do not have a client for whom you have supplemented their internal capabilities with a certified chemicals service. What could you do? Well, if you had a client who handled his basic lawn care himself but also handled the chemicals himself, yet you did business with him in another supplemental capacity, such as in our tree example, you could cite this client to demonstrate your supplemental service capabilities. Or, you could select another account for which your core service included both mowing and chemicals, even though this was not a competitive situation when you arrived on the scene. Perhaps your parents needed the combined mowing and chemicals service, and like any good parents, they gave the business to you as soon as you opened your doors.

So, let's take a look at what you have accomplished at this point. The first reference story gives you the ability to supplement an existing solution and the second us the ability to demonstrate chemicals expertise. Together, they show your ability to supplement using chemicals. You have *synthesized* your credibility.

The Limitations of "Supplementing"

Because of the nature of the competition objection, there is an inherent limitation that you should be aware of. In certain businesses, it is not possible to supplement, as I have described above, either because of the service or product you provide or the nature or capacity of the prospect's business. A good example of this is, say, you are selling payroll services to small businesses. The prospect is likely to use either your payroll service or mine. The prospect will not use both because the various segments of payroll service must be linked.

Even when you cannot actually supplement the competition, you still can use the words: *supplement, complement,* or *in addition to.* In this instance, you are not talking about a supplemental service, such as a pension-plan maintenance capability, which some payroll service providers offer their customers along with their payroll service. When you use the supplemental argument here, you do so as a way of sidestepping any direct comparison of services.

This letter strategy is difficult to follow when you first start to use it. This is because there is a small element of nontruth in your "supplemental" argument. However, remember that you are not overselling your solution and promising the client elements of the solutions that your company cannot deliver. Rather, you are using the supplemental argument to gain your first face-to-face meeting with the prospect. This is your only alternative to get the meeting. The way I justify this in my mind is that I am not overpromising on the solution delivery, but rather I am using the argument to gain the meeting. The meeting is the only way to understand the customer's need so that you can add value to their business. It is the incremental value I use to offset the small nontruth in using the supplemental argument. Rather, you try to get deeper into the sales process via an in-depth needs analysis based on the Meeting Management Worksheet (see Chapter 5) so that you can add enough value to your solution to justify any change in supplier.

Remember that any time a customer makes a change of vendors, there is cost involved, so your proposed solution must be superior under these adverse circumstances.

The "Will It Work?" Objection

When the sales prospect counters with the "Will it work?" objection they often mishandle their response and consequently lose the sale. Yet this objection is a close relative of the competition objection, in that the nature of the sales response is critical. Again, the challenge is to not offend the person you are speaking to.

In essence, the "Will it work?" objection asks the question, "If I buy from you, will the transaction be successful for me and my company?" It comes laden with prior bad experience, and is a question that carries a lot of baggage, including skepticism. Remember that confidence is the foundation for most successful sales transactions, so your response to this question is very important. You can't just assume "it will work"; you must assure the prospect that it will work.

Consider my business—sales training—to see why this is so important. If I were to deliver a sales training program for X company, the company would pay me at the completion of the period—say, within 30 days. The problem with that type of transaction is that the customer has only 30 days within which to measure the effect of the training program. Yes, the impact of any program is partly a function of a company's willingness and ability to implement the ideas presented in the program, but it is also partly a function of the quality of ideas presented. Suppose the company were willing and able to implement, but the quality was lacking. I would have gotten some of what I wanted out of the sales relationship (i.e., payment for my work), but the company will not have gotten what it was looking for from the relationship (i.e., an increase in sales). This is one of the reasons prospects use the "Will it work?" objection. There is always some concern on their part that what they are buying will not give them the results they want—or what the sales person promised.

This phenomenon is not specific to sales training, of course. It is a component of almost every purchase. If I buy a car, the dealer gets his money before I get my car. Will the car work? The dealer has already been paid! If I buy a new server for our company, the computer company gets its money before I get my new server. Will the server work? The computer company already has my money. Even if I go to the movies, the theater gets the money before I get to see the movie. If the movie is not as advertised, that becomes my problem—not the problem of the theater that sold me the ticket. Because of this pay-now, use-later format of a purchase and sales transaction, you can understand the purchaser's concern. If she buys from you, will she receive all of the benefits that you have promised? The obvious response will do little to advance your cause.

As I mentioned earlier, the source of this question may be a prior bad experience. That is, the prospect may be saying, "We have worked with your company in the past and we did not have a good experience." Of course, this may pre-date your employment with your company, but nonetheless, you are associated with prior bad experience and now need to respond.

A typical response is to tell the customer how the company has changed since then. You could point to process-improvement programs that have been implemented, you could highlight the new technology that has been deployed to automate manual systems and eliminate human error, and you could go so far as to imply that your sales predecessor was not effective and that is why you are here now. I can't say that all of these responses will hurt you because I don't believe that they will.

The intellectual metaphor that I use for the "Will it work?" objection is that on the "credibility scale" on which customers are constantly evaluating sales professionals, your responses will rank your credibility as relatively low. The scale ranges from minus 10 to positive 10, with minus 10 being the worst possible credibility rating and 10 being the best. On this scale, all sales professionals start at minus 10, because the negative image of the unscrupulous "used-car salesman" dominates the customer's thinking. The used car salesperson is typically known as a sales person who will literally say or do anything to win the business. We in the business know that this couldn't be further from the truth, but that does little to change the impression of most whom we meet for the first time.

When you tell the customer how much your company has changed, you have a positive impact; however, don't overestimate the value of what you are doing. Even if you say all of the right things, the best you can do is move from minus 10 to zero on the credibility scale. To really have an impact, to move all the way to plus 10 on the credibility scale, you must make extensive use of reference stories. As discussed earlier, a reference story is an example of how you faced a similar challenge and how you met that challenge with skill.

In fact, you can never have enough reference stories at your command, because a reference story is, in my opinion, the single best sales tool in the world, bar none. There is no explanation of new processes or examples of higher productivity levels with as great an impact, and there is no stronger marketing piece, in whatever format, that can take the place of a success story. For each given business problem you should have one, if not two, reference stories that demonstrate successful transactions.

As an example, consider this "Will it work?" objection: Suppose a customer tells the sales person that he worked with your company in the past and had a bad experience. Here's the recommended response:

"I can understand how you feel. That is a critical concern and I would feel exactly the same way if I were in your position. What I would like to do is give you the names and numbers of two customers who were in a similar position to you and for whom we developed great solutions. Their solutions are similar to the one that you are seeking, which is why I selected them for you. In addition, you might want to be aware of the new technology that we just deployed that will also help us be more successful in this area."

Any world-class response to this objection type must contain a reference to at least one example that is similar in most ways, so that you can move forward with this transaction. In this model response, you see that it includes the reference story. You also see that it includes mention of the improvements, acknowledging the customer's prior bad experience. Note also the placement of the reference story well ahead of mention of the process improvement, indicating which is the more important item in the response.

There are variations on the "Will it work?" objection that are more subtle, such as:

❏ Have you ever done this before in our industry?

❏ Do you have any prior experience working with our company?

❏ Have you ever worked with a company as large as ours?

❏ Have you ever worked with a company as small as ours?

In each case, your ideal response is the same as above—cite relevant reference stories and provide assurance of positive changes in your company's delivery of services or goods.

The "Not Now" Objection

And now, for the objection type that really makes the Goldner objection-handling model shine.

As a sales person, how many times have you heard prospects say:

❏ I don't have time for that now.

❏ I don't have a need for that now.

❏ I don't have a budget for that now.

❏ Send me something in the mail.

I'm sure you are quite familiar with this objection, especially if you work in telesales or if you do telephone prospecting to get an appointment while working in field sales. The "not now" objection typically comes into play when you call a prospect and either ask for an appointment (if you are in field sales) or ask for an extended telephone sales discovery session (if you work in telesales).

There are probably any number of ways to respond to this objection type, but let me show you the one that has the greatest impact. Suppose you just made the call and the person on the other end says, "We have no budget for your product or service." Your response should start with:

"I can understand that you don't have a budget at the moment. However, things are always changing—that is, sometimes you will have a budget and sometimes you won't have a budget. As long as I have you on the phone, do you mind if I ask you a few questions so that when you do have a budget, I will be well positioned to serve you?"

Why pursue a track like this, given that the prospect has just said he has no budget? The answer is simple, but it is best illustrated by an example. In the late 1990s, I was working with one of the largest and most successful international airlines in the world. They were not headquartered in the United States, but I was working with their North American sales organization. With respect to their target market in the United States, they sold "international travel"—that is, they did not have domestic U.S. routes but they did have international routes—say, from New York to London or San Francisco to London. I was helping their North American sales organization to transition from a channel-based approach to a direct-sales approach for top corporations in the U.S. market. To be successful, the sales force had to know how to prospect.

So here we were, calling upon the largest corporations in each of the 20 top markets in the United States to sell them tickets for international travel. One typical response was, "We don't have a need for international travel." At the time I thought it quite peculiar for global corporations to say they did not have a need for international travel. How did they visit their branch locations? Even with the best management system in the world, executives need to visit their international operations occasionally.

Our assessment of the situation was that they were probably indicating satisfaction with their present means of ticketing. So, here we were, hearing what sounded like the "not now" objection when, in fact, it was possibly the competition objection. But though I felt we were "possibly" getting the competition objection, we couldn't jump to conclusions and start talking about how we could supplement their existing relationships. That would be presumptuous. Instead, we did what well-trained sales professionals do when they don't understand what is happening: start the sales discovery process. This is the same sales discovery process that was discussed in Chapter 5.

If, as in this example, you need to enter the sales discovery process in order to react to the "not now" objection, there is a strong probability that the person on the other end of the line will answer in the affirmative and let your ask a few questions. By asking your sales discovery questions even though the prospect does have a budget in place, you will be one step closer to understanding their business. The only issue here is how many questions you should ask at this preliminary stage. My recommendation is three—the first three questions of the sales discovery process. Ideally, your goal is to set up a meeting at which you can pry open the box of possibilities that currently has been labeled "no budget." The "not now" objection can become the "yes now" situation if you can engage the prospect in the sales discovery process. And if all your attempts at conversation fail, ask if they would be interested in being put on your mailing list. For example,

> "I understand that the time is not right for you to meet with me now, but I wanted to thank you for allowing me to ask you a few questions. Would you mind if I kept you on the mailing list and touched base with you from time to time to reassess your needs?"

Believe it or not, the person at the other end invariably responds yes to this suggestion. They are looking to get off the phone, and you have just given them permission to do so. Once you have received the "mailing list" approval, or have agreed to "touch base every now and then," you can follow the ABC Call Cadence discussed in Chapter 4. When you do follow up at a later time, you can use the following response:

> "When we last spoke on [cite date], you asked me to touch base with you from time to time to reassess your needs. That's why I am calling you today."

Not only is this an effective approach, but you will start to notice that people tend to remember you based on these calls, even if they don't actually recall asking you to keep in touch. You are starting to build what I call "prospecting rapport." This strengthens each time you call, even when you leave a voice mail message. The prospect starts to remember having a relationship with you, even where one does not exist.

That is one scenario of the "mailing list" response to the "not now" objection. There's a variant on this response that, at the same time, opens the door just a crack. To show you the real power in this approach, let's say that with the "not now" objection comes the reply that what you are saying sounds interesting, and the prospect asks you to send them something in the mail so he can study it at leisure. In most instances, the person is saying that without any intention at all to read what you will send. Sometimes prospects say this to get you off the phone— but sometimes they genuinely want to read it later. You have a choice. You can play along with the prospect as if you don't know what is going on—or you can jump-start the sales process with a better response. Without seeming too shocked, say the following:

"I would be happy to send you something in the mail about that, but before I do, would you mind if I ask you a few questions? We happen to have a number of different things that I could send you and I want to be very precise that what I send will address your specific concern."

I hope that you can see how it's possible to overcome the "not now" objection. The model is both flexible and impactful. I don't think you can do much better than that!

* * *

Now, so far I've discussed how to respond to the "no budget" version of the "not now" objection. What if the variation you hear is the "no need" reply? The only difference between the "no need" and "no budget" is the word following the "no." Likewise for the "not now" and "no time" variations. Your response to the "no need" variation on "not now" could be as follows:

"I can understand that you don't have a need at the moment. However, things are always changing—that is, sometimes you will have a need and sometimes you won't have a need. As long as I have you on the phone, do you mind if I ask you a few questions so that when you do have a need, I will be well positioned to serve you?"

The response to the "no time" is similar:

"I can understand that you don't have the time at the moment. However, things are always changing—that is, sometimes you will have the time and sometimes you won't have the time. As long as I have you on the phone, do you mind if I ask you a few questions so that when you do have the time, I will be well positioned to serve you?"

In each case the script ends with your asking the prospect if you can ask additional questions, which help you determine whether the prospect's needs could be served by your solution. You have turned the "not now, no need, no time" objection into the beginning of the sales discovery process.

The Objection-Handling Matrix

I started this chapter by telling you that everything you have learned about handling objections, while it is good information to have, this probably is not the best option you have. Instead, I have described the four basic types of objections and how to handle them. Figure 6.1 presents those four types of objections within both selling and prospecting contexts—the two situations in which you will encounter objections.

Each objection type in the figure includes a "statement" that is a typical customer or prospect reaction, as well as your typical "response" or course of action. Presented in matrix form, the

FIGURE 6.1 Objection-Handling Matrix

Selling Objections	Prospecting Objections	
Price Objection ■ Statement ❖ Your price is too high ■ Responses ❖ Value ❖ Lowest total cost of ownership	**Competition** ■ Statement ❖ We're happy with our current provider ■ Responses ❖ Compliment ❖ Supplement	First in Sales Cycle
Will it work? ■ Statement ❖ Do you have experience in our industry? ❖ We've had bad experiences with your company in the past ■ Response ❖ Use relevant customer reference stories	**Not now** ■ Statement ❖ No need, interest, or budget ❖ Send something in mail ■ Response ❖ Use questions to get appt.	Second in Sales Cycle

figure differentiates between those objection that typically come earlier in the sales cycle versus those assumptions that came later in the sales cycle.

As discussed in earlier chapters, the prospecting phase of the sales cycle always comes first and ends with the agreement for additional contact—a face-to-face meeting if you are a field sales person or a telephone sales discovery session if you are in telesales. The selling phase commences immediately at the end of the prospecting phase. When you are telephone prospecting, the most likely objection you'll hear is the competition objection, with the "not now" objection a close second, so you should clearly prepare for both. In the selling phase, you typically receive the price objection before the "Will it work?" objection and can prepare for them in that order.

So, Figure 6.1 is a summary matrix that you should commit to memory—or at least refer to it often until you know it by heart. Having this model always in mind will make dealing with prospects' and customers' objections easy. My general guidance is to try to overcome an objection twice if you are in the prospecting phase because otherwise you will have a time-management issue. After two bona fide tries, place the prospect back into the sales cycle for follow-up later. In the selling phase of the sales cycle, however, you should try a lot harder to meet those objections head-on, because you are much further along in the sales cycle. You have much more to gain and lose, depending on the outcome of your discussions. And, of course, once again, the topic of preparation is at hand. Preparation permeates every aspect of sales, so you might as well get used to it and submit to its requirements.

*　*　*

This brings us to the end of the Execute stage of the Red Hot Sales process (Plan, Execute, Close). To summarize, this middle stage has three steps: *prospecting*, which you prepare for with a basic prospecting script; *selling*, which you prepare for by completing the Meeting Management Worksheet and composing six open-ended questions; and *objection handling*, which you anticipate by having a good response to each of the four objection types. This means that you are prepared for just about anything you will encounter up to this stage of the process. Yes, it is that easy if you want it to be.

Let's move on to Part III of the book, "Closing Strategies That Win the Business." There, I discuss how to prepare and deliver sales presentations and proposals with a great impact, as well as how to close the sale—of course, using 21st-century techniques.

Closing Strategies That Win the Business

CHAPTER 7

Closing the Sale
The Best-Kept Secrets

As I mentioned in earlier chapters, sales planning is clearly one of the key elements of a successful sales process. Like my mother, or like Curly in the movie *City Slickers*, I hold up that one finger, saying "I, too, know what the key to sales success is." It only makes sense: thought plus activity yields far greater results than just activity alone. That is why you plan—you plan so as to optimize the impact of your sales efforts.

But why discuss planning in a chapter on closing techniques? Because planning, if properly implemented, is a powerful closing technique! Proper sales planning and proper sales execution can do more for your sales results than any "closing technique" I am aware of. *Planning* is the best kept secret of closing the sale.

Sales Planning as a Closing Technique

Proper sales planning and proper sales execution can increase your chances of success at each step in the sales cycle, thereby helping you increase your chances of winning the business at the end of the sales cycle. But let's see exactly how sales planning can have that significant and positive impact on your sales results.

Remember the prospecting business plan presented in Chapter 1 (see Figure 1.2)? Built into that plan is a series of inter-dependent sales relationships that are collectively called your sales process. Starting at the very beginning of the sales process, you see that there is a relationship between completed calls and dials made. Moving to the next steps in the sales process, you see also that there is also a relationship between meetings scheduled and calls completed, a relationship between opportunities required and meetings scheduled, and finally, a ratio between sales achieved and opportunities required.

Figure 7.1 shows these relationships as a cycle of ratios—3 to 1, 4 to 1, and so on. Note, however, that the ratios in Figure 7.1 are different from those in Figure 1.2. This is because everyone's

FIGURE 7.1 Interdependent Sales Relationships

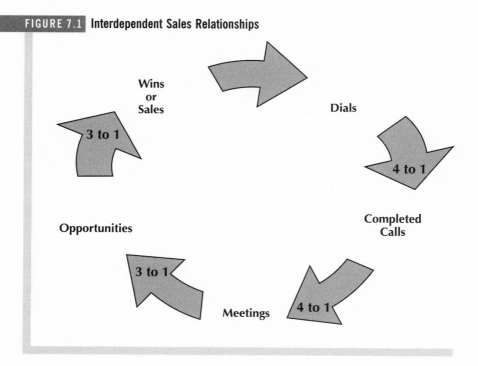

ratios or relationships will be different, depending on your selling skills, your company's position in the market, your product's position in that market, the economy, the extent to which you plan, the extent to which you execute, and possibly other factors. Irrespective of what your ratios might be at this point, you need to understand that these relationships underlie your respective sales processes. It is also important to understand that you can impact these ratios by both proper sales planning and proper sales execution. And, just to repeat, these are the first two stages of the Red Hot Sales process.

Part I divided the discussion of planning into three chapters—on prospect planning, territory planning, and account planning. If you take a look at Figure 7.2, you will see examples where and how each element of the sales planning model impacts your ability to close a sale and reach your sales goals.

FIGURE 7.2 How Planning Impacts the Closing

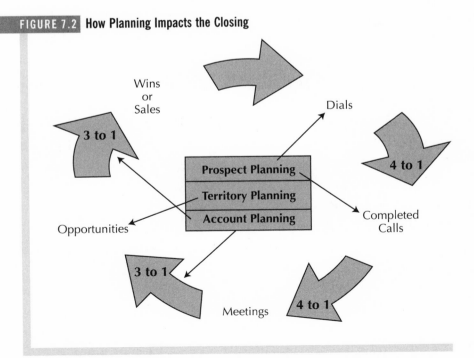

Prospect Planning for Greater Leverage

One major goal of the prospect planning process was to ensure that your time and effort were properly invested in developing new business activity. Stated simply, the goal is to be certain you are making enough dials or placing enough effort on the sales-development process to reach your annual sales goals. For example, you could ask a customer "Would you prefer to get started this week or next?" This is a traditional closing technique, known as the "alternative close." The idea behind it is to lead the customer to select between two alternatives (starting this week or next), thereby assuming that the sale has been made. This may be preferable to asking the customer directly if you have won the business. However, if you have not put the proper effort into the sales process to begin with, this closing technique probably will not work.

Please don't misconstrue what I am telling you. We still need to use a closing statement such as the Alternative Close in our sales process. We will discuss why later in this chapter. However, closing is not at the heart of the sales process as it has so often been portrayed historically in some of the older sales approaches.

In the movie made of the David Mamet play *Glengarry Glen Ross*, there is a famous (de)motivational speech given by Alec Baldwin, as the sales manager known only as Blake, in which he repeats the phrase "A-B-C" or "always be closing." The problem with an "always be closing" approach is that it assumes you have done everything else properly up to this point. Yet without proper sales planning, and without proper sales execution, you can make no such assumption.

Another drawback of the alternative close is that it leaves no room for negotiation. That is, there is no leverage in that type of closing statement. Assuming that you decide to use the alternative close on your next prospect, and you do a poor job of implementing it, you may not close the sale at all—and you risk losing future business as well. If this happens, you will likely go back to your office, figure out what you did wrong, practice a bit more, and then possibly do it correctly the next time.

Again, the leverage in this approach is limited. You can only inspect one or two sales. Contrast this to what I will show you next about planning, and you will see what I mean by "leverage."

Territory Planning at the Closing

If you recall from Chapter 2, territory planning is largely one of following the large-account strategy, which involves selecting the set of accounts that will maximize your sales results. Figure 7.2 illustrates how selecting the optimal set of accounts will increase your opportunity size, while selecting the wrong set of accounts will make you work a lot harder than necessary to achieve your sales goals. That's because the wrong accounts will decrease your average opportunity size and, as a result, you will need more opportunities to reach your sales goals.

Selecting the right set of accounts will also impact your average sales size. I did not show this impact in Figure 7.2 because it would complicate the diagram more than is necessary. Suffice it to say that an increase in your average opportunity size will likely have a similar impact on your average sales size.

The Account Planning Carryover Effect

The third element in the sales planning process is account planning, as discussed in Chapter 3. This planning is founded on a key concept: having a comprehensive sales process, in which the focus is expanded from the traditional purchasing and technical influences to include the economic and end-user influences. With a comprehensive understanding of the prospect's needs, you are more likely to identify the solution and an opportunity to close the sale should arise. Figure 7.2 shows how a comprehensive sales process positively impacts the likelihood of identifying an opportunity during the face-to-face meeting. (Again, the greater likelihood of winning a sale has not been depicted here, largely to keep Figure 7.2 as clear as possible.)

The Leverage Effect on Overall Sales

Now we are ready to look at Figure 7.3, which shows why sales planning is an extremely effective closing strategy. The left-hand column shows the elements of the sales process, as before. It also includes the ratios that were used in Figures 7.2 and 7.1. Columns 1, 2, and 3 to the right are a series of scenarios that demonstrate the effectiveness of this model.

Column 1 represents the "no prospecting" plan. Let's assume that you decide to make five dials per day, as you have

FIGURE 7.3 Impact of Planning on Sales Cycle

	Column 1 No Prospect Plan	Column 2 Prospect Plan	Column 3 Prospect, Territory, & Account Plan
Dials per day	5	10	10
Dials per year	1,250	2,500	2,500
Completed calls (25% per Figure 7.1)	313	625	625
Meetings (25% per Figure 7.1)	78	156	156
Opportunities (33% per Figure 7.1)	26	52	78
Closed sales (33% per Figure 7.1)	9	17	26
Average sales size	$100,000	$100,000	$125,000
Total sales for year	$900,000	$1,700,000	$3,250,000

done in prior years. Using the ratios established earlier, you see that such an approach would yield annual sales of $900,000.

Column 2 represents the prospecting plan alone. Using the same ratios as before, you see that the difference between having a prospecting plan and not having a prospecting plan is higher numbers for the necessary dials, completed calls, meetings, and opportunities. In essence, the prospecting plan told you that you had to place more of an effort to the sales process than you did in prior years. As a result of having a prospecting plan, you were able to increase your sales by $800,000 to $1,700,000. Assuming a commission rate of 10 percent, you would have effectively been paid $80,000 to complete your prospecting plan!

Column 3 represents having all three plans—prospecting, territory, and account. By having good plans and using the large-account strategy to select the "best" accounts, you were able to increase your average opportunity size and your average sales size by $25,000, to $125,000. You were also able to increase the rate at which you identified opportunities in your face-to-face meetings with customers. Prior to implementing those account plans, you were able to identify an opportunity one-third of the time. That means that three face-to-face meetings with customers and prospects would, on average, generate one opportunity. Indeed, by implementing your account plans, you were able to increase this ratio from 1 in 3 to 1 in 2. This means that instead of its taking three meetings to identify one opportunity, it took you only two meetings.

I did not differentiate the impact of the territory plan from that of the account plan, but you should realize that both have their own, separate impacts on your sales results, in the same way as did the prospecting plan. What is important here is to see that the sales results, after implementing the territory plan and account plans, yields an incremental sales result of $1,550,000, to $3,250,000.

Assuming that your prior year's sales results were $800,000, you could look at Column 1 and say that a $900,000 result is quite good. After all, your sales increased by 12.5 percent. However, by also implementing the planning tools, your sales results can increase by a little more than 300 percent!

This is what I mean by leverage, and these results show why sales planning and sales execution are the best-kept closing secrets in the world. Most sellers will practice their standard closing techniques and follow Alec Baldwin's recommendation to "always be closing." I, on the other hand, recommend a different approach. The proper closing technique can only impact the current sale when you have already properly executed the planning approaches. Remember, sales planning impacts everything that you do for the remainder of the year. That is true leverage!

Sales Execution as a Closing Technique

Part II of this book covered three topics: prospecting, sales discovery, and objection handling. Figure 7.4 shows the leverage effect that proper sales execution can have on your sales success. That is, using the prospecting techniques presented in Chapter 4 will increase the number of sales discovery meetings that you have each year. Using the sales discovery techniques presented in Chapter 5 will increase the number of opportunities that you identify each year in those meetings. Finally, developing sound objection-handling skills, as presented in Chapter 6, will increase the number of sales that you close.

Figure 7.5 shows the positive impact of this execution on your sales results. In short, I've added a Column 4 to Figure 7.3, as shown now in Figure 7.5.

In summary:

FIGURE 7.4 How Sales Execution Impacts the Closing

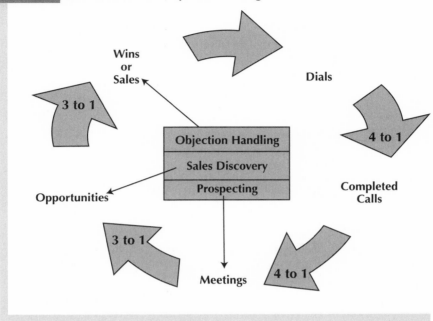

FIGURE 7.5 Impact of Execution on Sales Cycle

	Column 1 No Prospect Plan	Column 2 Prospect Plan	Column 3 Prospect, Territory, & Account Plan	Column 4 Improved Sales Execution
Dials per day	5	10	10	10
Dials per year	1,250	2,500	2,500	2,500
Completed calls	313	625	625	625
Meetings	78	156	156	208
Opportunities	26	52	78	83
Closed sales	9	17	26	33
Average sales size	$100,000	$100,000	$125,000	$140,000
Total sales for year	$900,000	$1,700,000	$3,250,000	$4,620,000

1. The ratio of completed calls to dials was left unchanged since this is a ratio that is partially impacted by skill and partially impacted by chance. Remember that the person you intend to call must be at his or her desk and taking calls when you dial, in order to achieve a completed call.

2. The ratio of meetings to completed calls was increased to 33 percent, owing to superior or improved sales execution.

3. The ratio of opportunities to meetings was increased to 40 percent, again owning to superior or improved sales execution.

4. The ratio of closure to opportunities was increased to 40 percent, based on improvements in sales execution.

5. The average sales size was increased to $140,000.

Based on your improved sales execution, you see a second leverage here, in the proper execution of the sales process. A leverage point gained in the sales process allows you to make one small change, such as asking high-quality, open-ended sales discovery questions at the start of your face-to-face sales meeting. This will mean you can reap significant benefits.

The figure again emphasizes how much your sales results can be improved, this time with good sales execution. As Column 4 shows, you improved sales results from $3,250,000, to $4,620,000.

Nurture, Not Closure

"Closing the sale" is not the guiding light to overall sales success, even if Alec Baldwin's character in *Glengarry Glen Ross* said you should "always be closing." I prefer not to use the word *closing,* as it implies an ending to the sales relationship. When you close a door, you place a physical barrier between your current position and your prior one. It is as if you are leaving off the past and starting anew somewhere else. The door is a metaphor for the end of a sale.

In Chapter 2, on territory planning, I told you that the secret to selling success was to focus on accounts that could produce a significant and continuing revenue stream. This is the large-account strategy. For instance, I have large accounts that do just this, and I am sure that you do, too. The beauty in having a large account is that you do not have to start from zero sales at the beginning of the month, quarter, or year. Rather, your large accounts provide a base of revenue that you can count on.

Many sellers I work with around the world all too often close a sale, celebrate their success, and then move on to their next prospect. It's as if they are closing the door on that last account in order to start a new relationship. In fact, it is said that more than 60 percent of customers change their sales relationship owing to perceived apathy on the part of the sales person. This "close and run" approach to sales only makes it more difficult for you to go back to those customers and build some more sales. Customers will remember your lack of follow-up and your follow-through indifference. Unfortunately, once you have damaged a sales relationship, it will take much time and effort to resume your position of grace with that customer.

A Step Toward Future Sales

Any experienced sales professional knows that it is much easier to sell additional solutions to the same customer than it is to find new customers and sell the first solution to them. For this reason, you cannot allow "closing a sale" to be the end of an account relationship. Rather, the closing should simply be a step to the further development of the account relationship. "Closing the sale" should only be the vehicle you use to reach to the next step in the account development cycle. It signifies a heightened awareness of one of the major goals of a sales professional: building account relationships.

The Consultative Sales Process

Now that you understand the true meaning of "closing a sale," let's consider exactly how to make that step toward future sales. The movie *Glengarry Glen Ross* presented the traditional view of sales, with the sales person attempting to close early, hard, and often. But because it's early, hard, and often, there is a good chance that the solution being sold is not right for the customer. That may also be why tactics such as the alternative close became so popular. If the solution is not right for the customer, but you keep on trying to move the process along to closure, you likely need a few closing phrases to do the trick.

My view of the sales process and the closing is more collaborative, as shown in Figure 7.6. The consultative sales process is how professional sales people align their interests with the interests of their customers—and how they ultimately close the sale.

As you can see in step 1 of Figure 7.6, there is a good chance that your interests as a sales person will be quite different from those of the customer. You are probably looking to close the deal and get as high a price as you can. The customer is also looking to close the deal, but looking to do so at the lowest price possible.

I have already shown that if the entire sales process is simply a negotiation around price, then the sales professional will be in a difficult position. Customers likely have the upper hand, as

FIGURE 7.6 The Consultative Sales Process

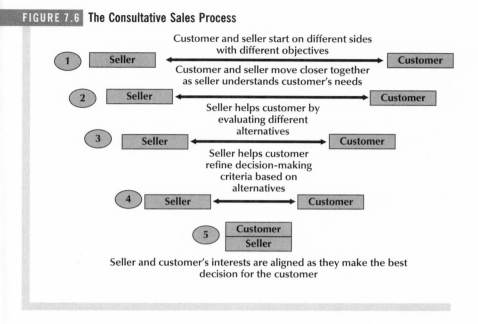

Customer and seller start on different sides
with different objectives

Customer and seller move closer together
as seller understands customer's needs

Seller helps customer by
evaluating different
alternatives

Seller helps customer
refine decision-making
criteria based on
alternatives

Seller and customer's interests are aligned as they make the best
decision for the customer

you are working in a competitive market where there are many alternatives. Most sales are awarded to the company or individual with the lowest price. The good news is that you need not accept this world, and that is why Chapter 5 discussed the questioning process for sales discovery. The main reason for asking those questions was to better understand the prospect's business and particular needs, as well as obtain information necessary to align your interests with those of the prospect.

Step 2 of the consultative sales process is to ask the customer a series of open-ended questions, such as those presented in Chapter 5. With those answers, you move to step 3 and begin to add value to the proposed business solution. In essence you are helping the customer better understand the options that are available. If there are no options, then you are in the commodity position and price will be the major determining factor in the sale. As a sales professional, you must always be able to see the options and bring them to the attention of the customer.

With step 3, you move to the position of consultant, helping the customer evaluate the different alternatives you have presented. The key here is to see the sale from the customer's point of view, matching your possible solutions to the customer's needs. It is important, however, not to push the customer, just offer clarification and guidance that helps make the best solution evident.

Step 4 takes you to the decision-making criteria. (If there are no options, then there is no need for decision-making criteria because there will only be one: price.) Again, it is your job to help the customer understand which criteria are best for his or her business. This usually involves sorting through the factors the customer has identified as criteria and ranking these so that the truly critical criteria stand out.

The Customer-Seller Partnership

It may seem odd to help the customer evaluate the options and determine the best solution for the business. After all, the customer is always trying to get a lower price from you and make your business less profitable as a result. You are the sales professional, supposedly selling the customer things he or she doesn't need and doing so at the highest possible price. Working on the same side as the customer probably seems like the Hatfields and the McCoys joining forces. As the sales professional, aren't you are supposed to be as far from the customer as possible?

Yet, Figure 7.6 shows you, not as enemies and not as magnets, but as two parties moving closer together to achieve a common good. In fact, that is what the consultative sales process is all about—and it's why you need to understand the value of the customer-seller partnership.

In many partnerships, such as a business partnership or a marriage, two parties come together for the betterment of both. When you are working with a customer, you need to acknowledge that the customer brings a lot of value to that partnership. The customer brings the knowledge that is required to get something accomplished in his or her business. You, the sales professional, may have the very best ideas in the world, but they will all be for naught if you don't understand how to make your solution work in the specific business your customer is in. That's why you need to work with the customer—as a collaborator and as a partner. Without the customer, you have little chance of making your solution work in that business.

However, if the customer could make that solution work on his or her own, there would be no need for you. All products and services could be procured over a Web site at, of course, the lowest possible price. Yet, you know this is not the case—that's why sales professionals like you are still part of the equation. The customer brings the internal knowledge to the relationship and you bring the external knowledge. Figure 7.7 highlights that customer-seller partnership.

Completing the Consultative Sales Process

Step 5 of the consultative sales process shows your interests and the customer's interests as aligned. The natural conclusion, or next step in the process, is for a sale to take place. The difference now is that it is in the customer's best interest to proceed; it is in your best interest to proceed, as well. And if it is in both parties' best interests to proceed, you might be wondering what is holding things up. The answer is nothing! Well, maybe I should have said almost nothing.

Let me first show you how it is that your interests and the

FIGURE 7.7 **The Customer-Seller Partnership**

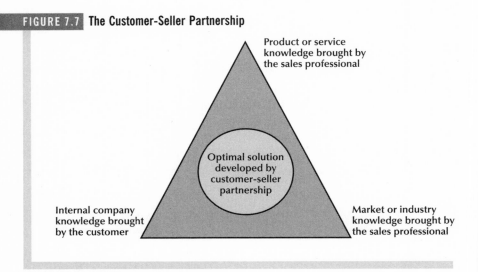

customer's interest can be 100 percent consistent. When you first approach a prospect, he or she has a budget in mind for your product or service, and also has a budget for the company as a whole. But when you add value to a customer's business through the consultative sales process, this not only makes the business more profitable, it also means that the budgets can grow as a result of your efforts. You can see this in Figure 7.8, with the "new customer budget" on the right-hand side of the chart. It is substantially larger than the "original customer budget" on the left-hand side.

If you do not add value and the customer's budget does not grow as a result, you are left working with a fixed budget and you have effectively created what mathematicians call a zero sum game. In a zero sum game, there must be winners and there must be losers. Sales professionals must avoid zero sum games at all costs!

It is easy to understand a zero sum game if you imagine a pie that you are going to share with your next-door neighbor.

FIGURE 7.8 Budget Growth Through Added Value

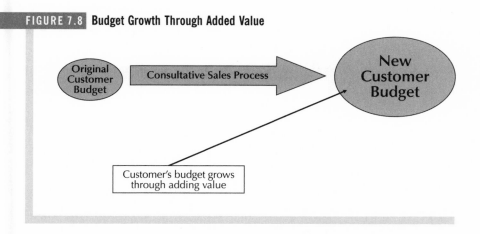

Assuming that the pie is relatively small, and that both of you are relatively hungry, you face the dilemma of how to fairly share the pie, given that splitting it in half will satisfy neither of your needs. That is, you will both still be hungry if the pie is split evenly down the middle.

So you begin to argue: "I want a bigger piece."

"No, I want a bigger piece," says your neighbor.

The problem is that the size of the pie is fixed, and so the larger your piece the smaller will be your neighbor's piece. You are in a zero sum game where there must be a winner and there must be a loser. The only way to fix the problems created by a zero sum game is to add something to the mix so that both parties can satisfy all of their needs. So, if your neighbor brings cookies or a sandwich to the table, your problems are solved. By bringing something else—otherwise known as adding value— the neighbor moves you both out of the realm of a zero sum game.

In a zero sum game, your *only* option as a sales professional is to expand the size of the pie by adding value. By not adding value, you effectively lock yourself into a zero sum game where you must be the loser. That is, if you take a lower price, you lose because you have lowered your sales margin and your company's profitability. If you close the sale with a higher price, you likely will damage the customer relationship and hence lose again.

No, the only solution to the zero sum game is to expand the size of the pie. When you add value to the customer's business, you expand the customer's budget and that expanded budget allows your interests to overlap. You can have a higher price for your solution (a bigger piece of the pie) while the customer can still receive a greater return on the investment.

The Closing Phrase

"If I buy from you, will it work?" This is, by far, your greatest impediment to closing a sale. As I explained in Chapter 6, most sales transactions are "pay now and see if it works later." It is this imbalance in the time it takes to realize the value from a transaction that makes a potential customer hesitant to move forward.

Believe it or not, this is when a good closing phrase comes into play. Even if you have done everything discussed in this book, and even if you have executed perfectly, the customer may still have a lingering concern. A good closing phrase or statement can help the prospect move forward with the sale.

A closing phrase or statement is not a means to force, trick, or intimidate a prospect into making a decision. Rather, it is simply the next appropriate step in a well-executed sales process. Figure 7.9 shows a variety of closing techniques and questions. My recommendation is that you take two of these and make them your own.

In a normal sales process, you reach a point when you feel it

FIGURE 7.9 .The Closing Phrase

- ■ The Opinion Close
  - • Do you feel that this makes sense?
  - • Does this make sense to you?
- ■ The Minor Point Close
  - • What would you like to see as the next step?
  - • When would you like to get started?
- ■ The Alternate Close
  - • Would you prefer to start this week or next?
  - • Can I expect your purchase order on Thursday or Friday?
- ■ The Summary Close
  - • Shall we give the credit department the go ahead?
  - • Would you like to get started immediately?
- ■ The Direct Close
  - • I'll process your order right now.
  - • I can have you approved in four hours.
- ■ The Fear of Loss Close
  - • If you don't move ahead now, I may not be able to meet your start-up schedule.
- ■ The Pending Event Close
  - • If you act now, I'll be happy to provide you an additional 5% discount.

is the right time to close the sale. You and the prospect are thinking the same way, talking the same way, and you both know it is time to proceed. The only thing the prospect will not do is clearly offer you the business. When you use a closing phrase or statement, only one of two outcomes is possible. The prospect will say yes and award you the business, or that prospect will render an objection. Chapter 6 identified the four objections and only two of these are likely to occur at closing: price or "Will it work?" In either case, you are prepared with a sound response. (Though the competition objection is also possible, it is more likely to occur during the telephone prospecting process.)

When you receive an objection at this point, it tells you that the prospect is still interested in your proposal, but you may not have answered all the questions. Take your time and respond to the objection to the best of your abilities. Then, use your second closing technique. If you receive a second objection, again respond to the best of your abilities. At this point, it is time for a third close, and I recommend that you go back to your original closing statement. It is okay to reuse your original closing statement at this point because you have separated your first use of it with an objection-handling technique, a second closing statement, and a second objection-handling technique. It will not likely sound redundant, but if you think it might, you can always integrate a third closing statement into your sales arsenal.

After your third attempt at a close, you face the same two outcomes. If you receive a third objection at this point, work with your customer to gain a better understanding of what is holding back the decision. It is likely to be more than a minor objection or a request for additional information.

*   *   *

For those who have worked in traditional sales, this chapter may have come with great surprises. You learned that sales planning and sales execution are the best closing techniques of all. You also learned about leverage, through which you can have a lasting and positive impact on your sales success—the large-account strategy is one such leverage point in the sales process. Finally, you learned how to use the consultative sales process to close your sales, resulting in a win-win outcome.

You also learned that even with the best planning and execution, you may still need to use a closing statement, such as the alternative close, in order to move the prospect over the threshold of indecision. The chapter provided seven possible scenarios for you. Next, we move to develop and deliver winning sales presentations.

CHAPTER 8

The Recipe for Winning Proposals

Let me start this chapter by stating something that you are probably going to feel is out of character for me: all sales proposals and sales presentations should be as standard as possible.

By "standard" I mean that as much content as possible in your proposals and presentations should be reusable. This is not to say that every proposal that you write and every presentation that you deliver should not be as customized as you can possibly make them. Your proposals and presentations should both be highly customized and standardized as much as feasible. How is that possible? Well, this chapter tells you how to make your proposals that very way. Chapter 9 tackles the presentation in the same manner.

The standard proposal format is presented in Figure 8.1. As you can see from the key at the bottom of the figure, various elements of the proposal are either standardized ("S"), customized ("C"), or both ("B").

FIGURE 8.1 **Standard Proposal Format**

- Introduction (S)
- The Customer's Needs (C)
- Your Solution (C)
- Why Select You? (S)
- Schedule of Events (C)
- Investment Summary (C)
- Reference Stories (B)

S – Standard, C – Customized, B – Both

The Introduction and the Customer's Needs

The first part of your proposal is the Introduction. It is a simple component, in which you thank the customer for giving you the opportunity to provide a proposal and you reference the meetings you have had during which you implemented your sales discovery efforts (see Chapter 5). A sample Introduction is presented in Figure 8.2 for your reference and future use.

The next section of your proposal details the customer's needs that you identified as a result of your sales discovery efforts. This is one of the most important segments of your proposal, so it is crucial you have done a great job of sales discovery.

One way to make this section really stand out is to present the customer's needs in a simple bulleted list. Key here is not to simply list the needs but, rather, to confirm that you have identified those needs in a comprehensive way. To do this, I recommend that you start with your key contact in the business for developing the list of needs, then review that list with each of the four buying influences in the company. (Your contact may

FIGURE 8.2 The Introduction Section of the Proposal

Dear Ms. Jones:

Thank you for the opportunity to work with XYZ Company ("XYZ"). During our recent meeting, you requested that we prepare a proposal to outline how the Sales & Performance Group could assist you in designing and delivering a sales training program for your upcoming meeting in June. This proposal summarizes our discussions and provides you with the requested information.

or may not be one of the four buying influences.) This will ensure that you have not only acknowledged these influences but also that you have included their needs in the sales process. If you do not have their needs listed in your proposal, it is unlikely your solution will speak to each of the four buying factors.

My vision of a proposal, therefore, is that there are four buying influences in any sale, and my proposal is a gift to the corporation (i.e., a business solution) that meets the needs documented by the purchasing team. The four buying influences have their own set of needs that are subsets of the primary business needs being addressed. One benefit of this model is that it helps you identify the definitive decision maker—typically the budget holder or economic decision maker.

The economic decision maker is the only one of the four buying influences who can say yes to the transaction. Any of the buying influences can say no to the sale, however, so it is important to manage all of the buying influences throughout the process. It is equally important that your proposal include an element of value related to each of the four buying influences.

Figure 8.3 is a checklist to make sure that your proposal is doing what it is supposed to do.

As an example, Figure 8.3 identifies each of the four buying influences for a particular customer, but note that the needs documented in the proposal are relevant to only three of these influences. Because any one of the buying influences can say no to a sales transaction, I must review my sales discovery process to identify the end user's needs. Knowingly submitting an incomplete proposal is not the best strategy, needless to say.

Once you have valid business needs for each of the four buying influences, merge those needs to produce a comprehensive list. Now, you can proceed to the next section of your proposal.

Your Solution

This is, of course, one of the most crucial sections of your proposal. It's where you have the opportunity to document and differentiate your business, based on stated needs. Notice that I said both document and differentiate.

FIGURE 8.3 Elements of Value for Each Buying Influence

BUYING INFLUENCE	YES/NO
Economic	Yes
End User	No
Technical	Yes
Purchasing	Yes

Remember the story about mushroom packaging in Chapter 5? The sales person found a way to solve a business problem for the customer by introducing a new concept—by differentiating his product from the competition. Basically, there are two types of needs—core and niche. Core needs are readily apparent and easily met—typically, the product or service that you sell fills a core need. But if all you are going to do is fulfill core needs, you are going to have a long and difficult sales career. The art of selling is in finding and then filling the niche needs of your customers.

In Chapter 5 of the sales discovery process, I gave you two basic questions designed to help you in this capacity. These value discovery questions were:

1. Given what you are doing now, are there areas for improvement?

2. Do you see any changes in the next six to twenty-four months that may impact your purchase decision now?

These questions help you identify niche needs, or those that do not have solutions readily available in the open market. Niche needs could be as simple as extended trade terms to allow the customer more time to pay for the goods and services, or something more complex like the implementation of a joint research and development project. Whatever the niche needs you have discovered in your sales discovery process, make absolutely certain that they show through loud and clear in your proposal.

Holding Onto Your Reader

You will work hours on your proposal, trying to get every aspect just right. The problem is that, no matter how hard you have worked, most clients will skip ahead to the last page of your proposal and read it backwards, looking for your pricing page. If your proposal fits within their price parameters, they may read further; if it does not, your proposal may get eliminated without the customer's taking the time to review the value points.

That's a pity because, if you are good at value selling, it is not uncommon for the value to be realized from implementation of your solution to exceed the purchase price of your proposal. Suppose, for example, your solution will cost $100,000; the savings that the company will realize as a result may easily exceed that amount. In truth, there are sufficient true cost savings realized from a business solution whereby the customer is, in essence, not paying for your solution at all.

Even if you don't believe that this can happen, you can envision a scenario in which your solution at least gives the customer the lowest total cost of ownership. The lowest total cost of ownership means that when you take the purchase price of your solution—say, $100,000—and deduct the cost savings associated with your solution—say, of $50,000—the true cost of your solution is less than the true cost of the competitive solution.

To finish illustrating this point, assume that the competitive solution will cost the customer $90,000. Here's where your difficulties begin. If all the customer does is turn to the last page of your proposal and see your purchase price of $100,000, and then compares that to the purchase price of the competitive solution of $90,000, that customer will in all likelihood select the competitive solution. This is the problem that occurs when customers read proposals backwards. How do you solve this problem?

Competing on Price Is Not a Sustainable Strategy

As I have said elsewhere in this book, winning your business by lowering your price is not good sales policy. Lowering your price does not require that you be a sales professional, and it does not require that you find that winning edge, that one small difference that makes you win the sale.

If you are a price-based sales person, start thinking about where all that price lowering has gotten you. About ten years back, AT&T and WorldCom were competing for the business of a particular global account. There was a lot at stake, and it was AT&T's business to lose. The opportunity was so large that the CEOs of the two companies got involved in the final sales negotiation. AT&T was the incumbent provider and was re-awarded the contract. After learning that they lost the business to AT&T, Bernie Ebbers, the CEO of WorldCom at the time, called the customer and said that he would beat any price that AT&T offered in order to win the business immediately. Not only would he beat the AT&T price, but he also agreed to replicate their solution, since the lowest price is not equal to the lowest total cost of ownership. As a result, the customer wanted to rescind its offer to AT&T and award the business to WorldCom, based on WorldCom's substantial price concession.

When AT&T's CEO learned of this, he went back to the customer and offered an even lower price than the one offered by WorldCom, without making any changes to the product or service levels built into the original solution. Keep in mind that this was a global account, and when these CEOs lowered their prices, the concessions amounted to millions—and possibly tens of millions—of dollars worth of savings to the customer. This was like two giant dinosaurs battling for the one remaining piece of food in their area.

Bernie Ebbers was an entrepreneurial CEO who had built WorldCom from the ground up by a series of mergers and acquisitions. He was not to be outdone, so when he learned about the new AT&T concession, he made yet another concession of his own, resulting in a price below what AT&T could deliver the business for. Presumably, WorldCom was also going to deliver the business at a loss. The customer had a ringside seat for this battle and re-awarded the business to WorldCom. At this point, I guess it was a matter of principle, as AT&T made another price concession, thus increasing its losses if it were to win the opportunity. After AT&T's second price concession, the company was awarded the business they had won originally, but at a much lower price.

From this story you can see that selling on the basis of price is not a good long-run, sustainable business or sales strategy. Yes, AT&T was able to sustain the losses on this one deal, but with too many deals like this even the largest corporation in the world cannot last. WorldCom ultimately went out of business in a blaze of infamy. I am not going to say that severe price cutting and selling at a loss led to its demise, but selling on the basis of price, selling at a loss, and ignoring a sound sales strategy, such as selling on the basis of value, contributed to its problems.

Raise Your Visibility as a Supplier of Niche Needs

To sell on the basis of value, you must raise the visibility of how you plan to fill the customer's niche needs. What I am about to tell you is one of the easiest ideas in this book to implement, and its impact can be huge if you implement it properly.

As mentioned earlier, the customer is likely to read your proposal from the back to the front so as to evaluate your price offer first. You cannot afford to let that customer read the proposal on his or her own terms, however. Rather, you present your proposal in a face-to-face meeting.

So, you complete your proposal and then call the customer

to ask for a meeting prior to your actually sending it in. Now, let's assume that the customer agrees to your meeting. You schedule the meeting for a day in the early afternoon, say around 1:00 PM. Then, when the customer asks to see the proposal beforehand, you tell the individual that you are still working on a few special elements that will be extremely valuable to the company when completed. Withhold sending the proposal until the evening prior to your meeting. Once you are sure that the individual is gone for the day, send the proposal via e-mail and apologize for the delay. Again, emphasize the special elements of the proposal that took the additional time.

The idea is to avoid their being able to read and analyze the proposal a day ahead of the meeting. Also, be unavailable in the morning on the day of your meeting—for that matter, be unreachable prior to the meeting. This situation makes it difficult for the customer to disqualify you on the basis of price. You cannot be available to cancel the meeting.

Show up at the customer's office at the appointed time and present your proposal as planned. By presenting the proposal in a face-to-face setting, you have the ability to address any price objections on the spot. You can also point to the niche or value points in the proposal and show that, while the purchase price may be higher than the competition's, your solution clearly gives the lowest total cost of ownership.

Use a chart such as shown in Figure 8.4 to compare your invoice price to the competition's price. In short, by controlling the environment in which the customer reviews your proposal, you have the best possible chance to sway the decision in your favor.

In Figure 8.4, the competition has value points of its own to contribute. Don't be so naïve as to pretend that your competitors

FIGURE 8.4 Lowest Total Cost of Ownership

ITEM	US	COMPETITION
Invoice or purchase price	$100,000	$90,000
Our value points	($50,000)	N/A
Their value points	N/A	($30,000)
True cost of solution	$50,000	$60,000

Lowest Total Cost of Ownership

cannot avail themselves of this same kind of sales strategy. But by giving customers credit for having creativity and "smarts" on their end, you come to an extremely important point.

Paul's Rule of One and Rule of Many

In *Red Hot Sales Negotiation*, I introduced Paul's Rule of One, which states: "Never let a negotiation deteriorate to only one item." Remember this rule, because when a negotiation narrows down to one point, typically price, you create an automatic win/ lose scenario for you. When you have no alternatives, you cannot trade a little more of one item for a little less of another. Paul's Rule of One has a corollary rule as it applies to sales proposals. Paul's Rule of Many states: "Never assume that the competition cannot add value to the customer's business, especially if it is the incumbent provider."

So, returning to Figure 8.4, you cannot assume that the

amount of the competition's value points is zero. The competition probably has the same opportunities to add value to the customer's business as you do. In fact, even if the competition doesn't understand what it means to sell value, the customer can impute a value to the competition that it may not even be aware of. Therefore, you want to develop as much value as possible.

What this means is that the $10,000 invoice price differential in Figure 8.4 is not your targeted value contribution. Using a rule of thumb that has served me well over the years, you triple-justify the invoice price differential between you and the competition. Again, using Figure 8.4 as our example, this means that your *minimum* target value contribution ought to be about $30,000. You might as well leave as little to chance as possible and add as much value as you can to the customer's business. In short, do the best that you can in every sales situation and don't just add the minimum value required to justify the invoice price differential.

Leverage the Cost of Switching Vendors

In 1992, our company won the global computer-training contract for Merck, the pharmaceutical giant. One of our sales professionals came up with a brilliant value contribution that saved Merck $2 million annually on the cost of processing invoices for computer training. There were other elements to the proposal and other value points that contributed to our solution, but this was the most impressive value contribution in the proposal.

In 1992, Bill Clinton had just won the White House. Hillary Clinton was appointed the task of formulating a plan for health care reform. Part of that proposed plan was to ensure that all Americans would have access to quality health care. If she were successful in her initiative, it could have meant that the pharmaceutical companies would be burdened with tremendous extra administrative costs. At the time, cost cutting was the major goal for all of the pharmaceutical companies. Our account manager developed a proposal with the centerpiece being a cost savings of $2 million annually, based on a consolidated invoicing solution she developed. We were not the incumbent provider in 1992, making our account manager's accomplishment even more impressive. She won the business from the competition by building a proposal using the same approach as the one presented in Figure 8.4.

Specifically, our invoice pricing was quite a bit higher than that of the competition; however, the account manager was able to overcome that obstacle by adding value to the customer's business. A portion of that price differential was justified by the $2 million in cost savings associated with her consolidated invoicing proposal, and the remainder by the other value points included in her proposal. She was clearly following Paul's Rule of Many.

The most important accomplishment in her victory, however, was to not sit back and rest on her laurels after winning the business. Rather, she studied exactly how she had won the business. As she developed a relationship with Merck, she was able to ask the customer questions that she could not ask otherwise. And one of the most startling of her discoveries was the cost to the customer of switching vendors. Figure 8.5 shows this most clearly. Any time a customer switches from one vendor to another, there are costs that must be overcome in order for a newcomer to win the business.

One of these costs is what I call accounting-integration costs, and these include the costs of developing and raising a purchase order, integrating your company's accounts receivable system and process with the customer's account payable system and

FIGURE 8.5 Vendor Switching Costs

ITEM	US	INCUMBENT COMPETITION
Invoice or purchase price	$5,000,000	$4,000,000
Accounting integration costs	- 0 -	($50,000)
Vendor-integration costs	- 0 -	($100,000)
First-year vendor mistakes	$100,000	- 0 -
True starting point for nonincumbent	$5,100,000	$3,850,000
True difference		$1,250,000

process, and costs associated with transaction approval and the payment process on the customer's end. Another set of costs include integrating the actual receipt of your product or service at the customer, the implementation of your product or service at the customer, and other costs associated with doing business with a new company in a given procurement area. Finally, any new vendor will make mistakes; these mistakes need to be accounted for as well.

What this tells you is that, when you are the incumbent provider, the business is yours to lose when that customer puts your business out for bid at the end of your contract. If you are not the incumbent provider, you need to work harder to justify the price differential, so apparent by comparing your invoice price to that of the incumbent's. Returning to Figure 8.5, you see what we might have been up against in 1992, in trying to win the Merck business from the competition. The competition's pricing was $4 million; ours was 25 percent higher, at $5,000,000. But as shown above, it is not sufficient to justify price differential alone. The competition is actually in a much better position to add value to the customer's business as the incumbent provider. They have the experience, they understand what is working and what is not working, they have access to all of the good information, and they have access to customer personnel.

If you are not the incumbent provider, assume that the incumbent is adding some value to the customer's business. Also assume that the customer is imputing more value than even the competition is aware of. (There has got to be a good reason the customer entered into an agreement with the competition in the first place—likely perceived value.) There also has got to be a good reason the customer stayed in the agreement with the competition for a year or more. The Merck agreement was a two-year agreement and if the incumbent provider were not doing a good job, the customer would have found a way to get out of the agreement earlier. Here again, by "good job" I am suggesting that the customer *believes* that the incumbent is adding value to its business.

Figure 8.6 shows the obstacles for a nonincumbent provider. In 1992, we not only had to overcome an invoice price differential, but we also had to overcome vendor-switching costs, competitive value points that carry over from one year to another (as

FIGURE 8.6 True Nonincumbent Proposal Challenge

ITEM	US	INCUMBENT COMPETITION
Invoice or purchase price	$5,000,000	$4,000,000
Vendor-switching costs	- 0 -	($250,000)
Incumbent value points—prior year	- 0 -	($100,000)
Incumbent value points—new		($75,000)
Subtotal	$5,000,000	$3,575,000
Your proposal hurdle		$1,425,000

many value points do), and competitive value points for the new proposal (because the competition knows that it, too, cannot rest on its laurels).

With these huge financial obstacles facing nonincumbent providers, I often find it humorous how some old-fashioned sellers believe that business is won and lost on a golf course or in a restaurant. I am not going to tell you that it is *not* important to have a good relationship with a customer. However, good relationships with customers come along after you have developed a proposal that accounts for all the factors presented in Figure 8.6.

Not Always on the Outside Looking In

The good news is that you are not always in an uphill situation. There are many times when you are the incumbent provider, and in those instances it is important that you call attention to the costs associated with switching vendors, as well as the risk inherent in working with a new company.

There is a cost to the customer when you are the incumbent provider, and that is the cost involved in renewing the agreement with you. For example, at the end of their two-year agreement with us, Merck wanted to know that they were still getting a good price—they wanted to test the waters and see what the competition could come up with. At least these are the two reasons that Merck gave us when we asked, "Why do you want to go to market after two years when you are so happy with our work?"

As we started to question the extent of the vendor-selection process, we learned that Merck would form a relatively large procurement team of five to ten people. The team would develop a request for proposal, or RFP; they would develop a vendor-evaluation format; they would read and prioritize a relatively large number of proposals; and they would listen to several finalist presentations. After this, they would agree upon a vendor and present their selection to a small management team, which would ratify the vendor selection.

When we estimated the time for all of the people involved, and estimated the salaries and overhead costs, we concluded that a vendor-selection process for a relatively significant proposal could cost in the range of $50,000 to $100,000. When you consider that a significant purchase could be in the $500,000 to $5,000,000 range, this is a significant premium to pay for the right to select a new vendor. If you take the annual customer budget, which ranges between $500,000 and $5,000,000, and break that budget down into underlying projects, a company could probably fund one additional project by forgoing the vendor-selection process. When you add this cost of vendor selection to the cost of switching vendors and the risk of doing so, a compelling argument can be made to extend an existing agreement with a supplier.

I point out these company costs for two reasons. First, you never know what will happen if you, as an incumbent vendor, make that argument to your customer. There is a good chance that the customer will agree with you. And, second, once you do the calculations for one customer, you can easily do it for any number of other customers you currently serve. Consistent with the concept of selling value, this is not an argument that you should reserve for the point of closing. This is an argument you want to make a full six months or more before the company's decision to issue an RFP.

Manage Customer Perceptions

In my book *Red-Hot Customers*, we devoted an entire chapter to the Ultimate Selling Tool. At its core, the Ultimate Selling Tool is a process that you can undertake to influence the customer's decisionmaking criteria. The process of writing an effective RFP and the process of developing an evaluation method are not trivial endeavors. At Merck, we found that they were willing to accept our counsel on how to handle these two important business processes. In fact, Merck considered our help an added value. This was when we realized that our help was the ultimate form of sales. To the extent that you can impact the customer's decision-making criteria, you approach the pinnacle of the sales process.

Throughout this book I have reinforced the concept that sales is the effective management of customer perceptions about what is important in a relationship. Your job as a sales professional is to get the customer to think. If the customer does not think, he or she will do nothing different this year compared to last year. If you are not the incumbent supplier, this means very little opportunity to break into the account. If you are the incumbent supplier, it means little opportunity to sell more this year than last year. Neither is a good outcome for you.

Thus, you need to get the customer to think properly, and by thinking properly I mean to align customer perceptions to the value points of your solution. This concept permeates this whole book. And like many other important points made in this book, it is a process that extends through the sales process. It is not reserved for the point of sale.

Why Select You?

The next section of the proposal is Why Select You? This is the time to remind the customer why your solution is preferable to that of the competition. As Figure 8.1 indicates, this section can be standardized and should be based on your five unique selling points. These were described in Chapter 5, in connection with the Meeting Management Worksheet. The only difference here is that, for the proposal, these selling points should appear in the customer's order of preference. I discuss this topic in greater depth in Chapter 9, dealing with the sales presentation.

Schedule of Events

This section of the proposal provides the customer with a plan for project implementation and at the same time sends a couple of important messages to the customer. First, it tells the customer that you have done this type of project before. Second, it tells the customer that you have given quality thought to the proposal.

A schedule of events reflects your business. Depending on the type of work that you do, the events in your schedule may be different, and may vary in the degree of detail, but the overall concept and reasoning are the same: you lay out for the customer just how you will provide the goods or services you are offering.

Investment Summary

The Investment Summary shows the customer that he or she will receive a good return on any investment with you. Part of this summary includes a survey of the competition, but bear in mind that you will have traditional, nontraditional, and internal competitors, as well as competition from the idea of "doing nothing."

Indeed, what most sales people fail to realize when writing a sales proposal is that they are competing not only against the companies they perceive as competitors, but they are also competing against all other uses of the funds that the customer might have available for the project. So, to be fully comprehensive, your list of competitors should include companies that sell noncompetitive goods and services, such as furniture or management consulting services. Even if you include all the other vendor types in your competitor list, you are not yet being fully comprehensive.

In addition to third-party vendors, remember that the customer could opt to invest the funds in human resources, by hiring additional people, or in physical resources, by building a new manufacturing plant. At least by including human and physical resources in your competitor list, you come close to achieving comprehensiveness.

Your last competitor, however, is the most difficult of all—the option to "do nothing." The customer always has the right to back off from your proposal, as well as the proposals from other companies that he or she purchases goods and services from. The customer can also put a hiring and spending freeze into place, limiting or closing off any ability to enhance even internal resources. If there are no good investment alternatives in the market, the customer may forgo all options and just leave the money in the bank.

Of course, when I say "leave the money in the bank," I don't actually mean a savings account, though that is one option. The entire range of debt and equity investment options are available, and your customer may choose to let the money grow rather than spend it on your product or service. Believe it or not, the "do nothing" alternative is your most difficult competitor to beat.

Figure 8.7 shows a list of typical competitors. The first three types of competitors are all similar, in that the customer has decided to invest in their own business by one means or another

FIGURE 8.7 Comprehensive List of Competitors

- Traditional, direct competitors; other companies in your business

- Nontraditional, indirect competitors; companies that produce goods and services for other uses by the customer

- Internal investment competitors; hiring of additional human resources or the investment in property, plant, and equipment

---

- Do Nothing. Investment in traditional financial instruments that yield a return, but a return that does not come from the customer's own internal production and sale of goods and services

to improve its return on investment. The fourth one is the "do nothing" competitor.

Comparing Investment Alternatives

Figure 8.7 is theory. Now, let's consider an actual example in which various competitors are compared. One of my past clients sold industrial sandpaper. A common application of industrial sandpaper is in the furniture industry; if you were a manufacturer of wooden tables, say, you would have to purchase industrial sandpaper for use in your factory, and the sandpaper would be used to smooth the table tops and table legs. When I started working with this client, I asked the person to describe the existing sales process. He explained that a sales person would walk into a furniture factory and speak to the factory foreman, claiming that this company's sandpaper was better than the competitor's sandpaper, which the customer was presently using.

To prove that my client's sandpaper was better, the sales person would set up a test. The first part of the test was to count how many table tops the competitor's sandpaper could sand before wearing out. Then, the prospect would use my client's sandpaper and measure the results. Then, to compare the two sandpapers to determine which product was better, the sales person divided the number of tables completed with each sandpaper by the cost of each product. The sandpaper with the larger result was the better sandpaper.

While this may seem like an unsophisticated approach to sales, it is one used in many industries. In fact, it is used in most manufacturing applications, most chemical applications, and in many technology applications. The method of comparison is unsophisticated, however, because it does not take advantage of what we have talked about in this book and it does not take advantage of what I am about to show you.

First, this approach is not *needs-based* and thus is not an application of the consultative sales process. Second, it is not *value-based*, as the sales person is focused only on the core needs of the customer. Third, and most important as it relates to this chapter, it considers only *one class of competitors*. To be a true sales professional, you must address all of the competitors identified in Figure 8.7.

The Only Way to Present Your Solution

Because you have four kinds of competitors, you must look for a common denominator, or one way to compare four disparate alternatives. When you consider only your direct competitors, as in the sandpaper story, you make head-to-head, or direct, comparisons. In the case of a sandpaper, the head-to-head comparison was done on a cost-per-unit-of-measure basis—which sandpaper is more cost-effective based on how long it lasts.

When you add the indirect competitors, such as a management consulting firm or a training program for your company (i.e., an alternative use of funds for the customer), you can no longer use head-to-head comparisons because a management consulting firm does not work on a factory assembly line in the way that sandpaper does. The same is true for internal investment competitors, such as adding an additional employee, and the "do nothing" competitor, investing corporate funds outside of the business. The only way to compare all the competitors is to measure them on a financial basis, or what is otherwise known as return on investment (ROI).

To calculate the return on investment for your product or service, you subtract the cost of your investment from the anticipated return. Then, you divide the result by the cost of the solution, to get a percentage that is the return on investment.

If you multiply the $1 million in annual sales by 10 percent, you come up with an increase in production and sales of $100,000. However, generally in manufacturing, the full value of incremental machinery sold cannot be counted because the customer also incurs incremental production costs. You must account for those incremental production costs in your ROI calculations, typically by 50 percent. Adjusting for the gross profit on manufacturing output by 50 percent, you will see that the true benefit to the customer is not the incremental revenue of $100,000, but rather the incremental gross profit on those sales of $50,000. (Remember that gross profit is defined as sales less direct cost of sales.) In this case, the direct cost of sales is the incremental cost the customer must bear in order to produce one more unit of its product.

In our example, let us assume that the cost of the equipment is $30,000. We now have enough information to complete the

ROI calculation, as shown in Figure 8.8. We take the return anticipated by the customer of $50,000, then deduct the cost of purchasing the machine at $30,000. The residual value after deducting the cost of the solution is $20,000. When you divide the $20,000 by the cost of the investment (i.e., the machine), the result is a return on investment of 66 percent.

A percentage return on investment gives you the opportunity to compare your solution to those of the direct competitors. More important, it gives you the opportunity to compare your solution to every other investment alternative. The common denominator is return on investment.

When preparing your Investment Summary, consider the following additional points:

❏ Never use the word *price* when presenting the investment associated with your product or service. Use the word *investment* instead.

❏ If the cost of your solution has several components, detail the different major cost elements and make them the first part of your Investment Summary.

FIGURE 8.8 How to Calculate ROI

Return anticipated from your machine	$50,000
Cost of your machine	$30,000
Return from your machine less cost of your machine	$20,000
Return on investment	66%

❏ After showing the customer how the cost or investment portion of your proposal is calculated, complete an ROI analysis.

Caveat: Avoid Customer Traps

Have you ever had a customer come back to you with an old proposal in hand? I have. I have had customers return with proposals that are a year old and older. They'll say something like, "Okay, we're ready to get started now!" The customer is ready to get started with a proposal that is quite out of date. Prices of your products and services may have changed, yet the customer is expecting you to honor the old price while you want to use your current pricing structure. This places you in a difficult position.

Sometimes customers will "cherry pick" your proposal. They give you a long list of items they are looking for, and they imply that they are looking to make a large acquisition. But what they are really looking for is to have a group of vendors—your direct competitors—all submit proposals giving the very best pricing, considering the implied magnitude of the opportunity. Then, they select a few items from each vendor, "cherry picking" the best opportunities. If there are three competitors and five products required, the customer selects two products from competitor number one, two products from competitor number two, and one product from competitor number three. When this happens, you are expected to supply the products assigned to you, at the prices you specified. In most instances, it is no longer a good deal for you.

The way to counter both of these customer tactics is to include two sentences at the end of your Investment Summary:

❏ prices in this proposal are based on selecting the entire proposal.

❏ prices are valid for a period of 60 from the date of this proposal.

You can set the period to any period you think is appropriate—30 days, 60 days, or more.

Reference Stories

The only thing missing from your proposal at this point is the Reference Stories. These stories lend credibility to your proposal. Your Investment Summary shows the potential of your proposal; the reference stories provide evidence that your predictions will come true.

There is only one valid way to address the customer's concerns about the potential return on the investment. The reference stories show similar circumstances when the return on investment did take place as anticipated. They are third-party evidence that your solutions work. They also provide a means for the customer to validate your arguments, by contacting prior customers and obtaining direct feedback. In general, provide two reference stories at the end of each proposal.

How to Synthesize a Story

When you have the perfect reference story for a customer, you are in great shape. However, reference stories have two requirements, both of which must be met for a story to be considered "perfect."

The first requirement is that your example be in the same

industry. Customers believe that their industry is unique. If you are proposing a solution for a law firm, the people at the firm believe that their needs are different from others' needs. If you have successfully installed your solution in other law firms, you have a leg up on the competition, so make sure you highlight this in your proposal. If your experience has not been industry-specific, you will have to synthesize your story.

The second requirement for a perfect reference story is similar geography. This is not as big an issue in the United States as it is in Europe, where there are a larger number of smaller countries, with differing cultures and traditions. However, even in the United States, geographic proximity is best.

If you do not have the perfect reference story, you can synthesize one, using two different experiences, each with one of the required traits. For example, you can merge the industry element from one story with the geographic element of another. I agree that a synthesized reference story is not as good as a perfect reference story, but a synthesized reference story is better than no reference story at all. Needless to say, a merged reference story counts only as one story, and so you need to include another as well.

The Best Reference Story of All

The best possible reference story is one from within the company itself. If you are developing a proposal for a global company, and you have done work with that company in another country, that is important for the customer to know. Even if your new proposal is for a part of the company in the United States, far removed from where you did the prior work, it will carry a lot of credibility. Also, global corporations typically have several lines of business, and a project completed in one area may well carry over to another. A global bank, for example, can have both consumer and corporate divisions. Even if your past experience is consumer banking, mention it in any proposal for work in the corporate division.

When you have an internal reference story, highlight that fact both at the beginning of your proposal and as your first reference story. This may be a good time to use three reference stories—two external and one internal.

New-Product Reference Stories

Another reference-story challenge that you are apt to face is when you have a new-product release. In the early days of a new product, you cannot possibly have reference stories regarding this product.

If this is the case, use past reference stories that show how well you introduced a new product. If you were able to be successful with past new-product releases, why wouldn't you be successful with this new-product release? In truth, all of your most successful products—the ones that you sell every day—were new products at one point or another.

One Last, Great Point: Limited-Access Proposals

Many times, larger companies and local, state, and federal governmental agencies elect to use a formal proposal process. I just completed a proposal like this that was issued by one of the largest U.S. insurance companies. The RPF process was done through an Internet procurement tool. It serves as a good example of this peculiar situation.

I received an e-mail telling me that the RFP was ready for viewing. I had two weeks to download the proposal and post my response. I was allowed to ask questions, but the questions had to be submitted online. I was not allowed to speak with any employees of the insurance company once the proposal was issued—direct contact with a company employee meant immediate disqualification.

When my questions were submitted online, both the questions and the company's answers were posted as well for everyone to see. While there were many questions on the proposal, the insurance company made it clear that price would be a major factor in the decision-making process. Because of the ban on direct communication, it was difficult to ask the typical sales discovery questions. And without the ability to ask questions, it was difficult to create a proposal that would differentiate my solution from those of the competition, and to add value to the customer's sales cycle. The customer was trying to commoditize my products and services, and they were doing a good job of it. How did I cope with this situation?

If you work with large corporations, as we typically do, this type of proposal process may seem familiar. If you work with governmental agencies, which are notorious for issuing RFPs with a strong price focus, this scenario will also be familiar. I have developed what I believe to be a unique way to respond. When faced with a low-information, high-price-focused RFP situation, I provide two solutions. The first solution is the one specified by the customer in the RFP, and it has a strong price focus. Then, I attach a second solution, even if it is not requested. This second solution contains my true recommendation—the solution I would likely have proposed if it were not for the customer's decision-making process.

The only time you cannot use a technique such as this is when the customer clearly prohibits it and doing so will disqualify your proposal. In most cases, I feel the effort is worth making. My first submission allows me to get to the finalist stage. The customer selects two, three, and possibly four competitors to go to the next round of procurement. Once in the door, I have the opportunity to do a proper needs assessment and can update and position my solution. This is where I really want to be.

* * *

This chapter helped you develop a high-impact proposal that will either win you the business or, more likely, move you to the next round of procurement—the final presentation. So, let's move on to that final chapter of Part III and learn how to develop a presentation that wins the business!

CHAPTER 9

Winning Sales Presentations

Now, you are at the end of the sales process: the finalist presentation. In this chapter, I show you how to convert your proposal into an effective sales presentation and win the business!

To Go First, or Not to Go First: That Is the Question

If we could speak face to face, I am certain we could debate this point for hours. The answer lies in the type of salesperson you are. If you are a price-based, transactional seller, you position your product or service as a commodity and so you want the opportunity to go last in every presentation situation. This way you are in the best position to beat the competition with a lower price. If you go last, you can always ask the customer what prices he or she has received from other vendors and then indicate your willingness to offer the lowest price.

This is not selling as I understand the word, but of course you know that by now, having read this book up to this point. In

179

fact, this kind of selling almost sounds like an auction, and auctions can be done on the Internet, without direct involvement of sales professionals. I do not advocate that you compete on the basis of price, although I do acknowledge that there are situations when you may need to use price as one element of your overall sales process. Some of these situations will be due to circumstances beyond your control, and others will be due to flaws in your sales process or sales strategy. Either way, competing on the basis of price is usually not the formula for a successful, long-run sales career.

If you are a value-based, relationship-oriented sales professional, however, you will want to always go first to make that presentation! In fact, you can almost make going first a condition of your delivering a presentation at all. When the customer lets you know that you are among two or three finalists, announce right then and there that you would like to go first.

The reason for going first is simple: you are well prepared. The preparation traces back to a point made in Chapter 5, on sales discovery. By asking a question along the lines of "What do you value in a relationship with a company like ours?" you probed for the customer's current buying criteria. Knowing the customer's criteria, you aligned those criteria with key value points in your solution.

Going first also sends the message that you have done a lot of hard work to develop the solution you propose. Likewise, it tells the customer that you believe in that solution and stand behind it. Going first also positions you as the vendor against whom all others will be judged. It says that you want to be the one to set the bar over which any other competitor must jump in order to win the business. By going first, you become the standard bearer for your business.

Polish Your Presentation Skills

I assume that you are familiar with the techniques of public speaking, to the extent that they apply to small-group presentations. This is not a book on public speaking. And if this is a weakness for you, you should consider working with a coach to develop your skills. For our perspective here, I give just a few tips.

To begin, you should divide the room into two, three, or four segments, depending on the size of the audience. Finalist presentations rarely exceed ten participants; if that is the case, three segments may be enough. One segment can be on the right-hand side of the room (from your perspective), one segment can be directly in front of you, and one segment can be on your left.

A standard presentation technique is to address each segment of the room in turn, starting on the right and moving to the center, and then to the left. The reverse also works just fine. By making eye contact with each room segment, you can ensure that you are drawing each person into your presentation. If you notice that someone is not paying attention, you can ask a general question to try to bring the individual back into the presentation. For instance, a question that requires everyone to raise his or her hand in agreement might be good at this point. This way, you do not have to focus on the person that is disinterested, but you can still get them involved in the presentation.

If asking a general question requiring everyone to raise a hand in agreement does not work, try asking a question directed at the inattentive person. Make sure it is a soft and easy question, as there may be a reason they are distracted and you do not want to alienate. You can also physically move closer to the person, gliding into his or her personal space, and gently remind the individual to pay attention to what you are doing—being careful, of course, not to alert the rest of the group or call out the individual.

In addition to segmenting the room and addressing each room segment in turn, you can specifically address each person as his or her need or objective is discussed. I remember people telling me about Frank Sinatra when they had seen him in concert. They typically saw him in a large concert hall such as the ones in either Las Vegas or Atlantic City. Yet each person described the experience in the same way. They all said that he made you feel as though you were the only person in the concert hall. That's exactly how you want each person to feel as you address their specific concern, objective, or need.

Always Be the Standard Bearer

Selling is all about setting, managing, and re-setting the standards or perceptions that customers have of what is important in a relationship with a company like yours. The customer usually enters a given sales transaction believing that he or she will select the company that will meet the current set of needs. Your job is to understand and then manage this belief until the customer's buying criteria align with the strengths of your solution.

The extent to which you can manage those customer perceptions and criteria is a function of where you enter the sales cycle. If you enter early, you have a lot of time to accomplish this, and time improves your chances of being successful in the sales process. If you enter in the middle of the cycle, not only do you have less time to manage customer perceptions but also the competition has had time to get involved. This complicates the picture for the customer and may be one reason that customers frequently revert to price as their key decision-making criterion. Everything else being equal, they select the least expensive solution. Fortunately, you have the ability to ensure that criteria other than price dominate the customer's decision-making process.

If you enter the sales cycle late, you are in a tough position. First, you have only limited time to manage customer perceptions. You can have little, if any, impact on the decision-making process. What's worse, there is a good chance that the competition has shaped those customer perceptions and you have to align your strengths to these competitor-based criteria. There is little, if anything, you can do at this point except to compete on the basis of price.

Ultimately, your best option if you frequently enter the sales cycle at the end is to ensure that you have a full pipeline of prospects to counterbalance your losses. If possible, don't put yourself in this position, whereby you rely on one or two opportunities to reach your sales goals. Since most customers have recurring buying patterns, entering the sales process consistently late is likely to lock you out of later sales as well. If you realize that your customer purchases items like the ones that you are selling, and you are not well positioned for the current sale, think about how to properly position yourself for the next sale.

First to Customer

Where you enter the next sales cycle and the ones that follow after that are a function of desire, process, and strategy. The fact that most customers go to market one or more times a year provides you with the opportunity to be "first to customer" in every sales cycle after the first sales cycle.

Being first to customer gives you the maximum time in each sales cycle to manage customer perceptions. Additionally, one sales cycle can blend into another over time, and so effective management of customer perceptions becomes an ongoing part of your sales relationship. Your job is to use the large-account strategy to select customers who will allow you to maximize your sales growth, then make managing customer perceptions a key ongoing responsibility. In so doing, you will see how much sense it makes to go first in every finalist's presentation you are part of. Being first to the customer to present your solution set is a powerful sales strategy.

Prepare a High-Impact Sales Presentation

The seven key elements of an effective sales presentation are presented in Figure 9.1. They include starting every sales presentation with a clear and concise summary of the customer's needs and objectives. Base this summary on the responses you got to the sales discovery questions as discussed in Chapter 5. It

FIGURE 9.1 Seven Points of an Effective Sales Presentation

- 1. Restate the customer's needs and objectives for seeking the solution you are providing.
- 2. Allow for customer participation to ensure that you fully understand and document the customer's needs and objectives.
- 3. Present your solution including a clear map back to the customer's needs and objectives.
- 4. Address anticipated customer objections.
- 5. Summarize why the customer should select your solution.
- 6. Provide the customer with a compelling reason to act now and in your favor.
- 7. Follow through with "zingers" from a media search tool such as Google Alerts.

is important, here, to let the customer know that you understand what he or she is trying to accomplish. It is also important to remind the customer why he or she is listening to your finalist's presentation.

Acknowledge Individual Interests

You likely will be giving your presentation to the customer's purchasing committee. Rarely, if ever, does a single person make these decisions today. Presumably, you have identified the four buying influences in the sales process, as they will likely be present when you make your presentation. You don't need to identify these buying influences by name, but one technique adds greatly to your success: assign each of the customer's needs and objectives to a buying influence. This way, you are addressing at least one need or objective for each of the buying influences.

Remember that any of the buying influences can kill your sale. It takes only one to vote against your proposal. Since you have a presentation that literally links their different objectives to particular components of your solution, it is as if you are offering gift-wrapped packages for each of the buying influences. You can be certain that everyone attending the presentation will be interested in what you have to say.

This approach clearly has some inherent assumptions. First, being able to address each of the buying influences assumes that you have met with them as part of your sales discovery process. You have obviously done something correct to reach this presentation stage; however, now you are competing against the crème de la crème, and you must be at your very best.

Second, you will have confirmed who will be attending your presentation. You should know the name, title, and key interests of each person present in the room. Why are they attending your presentation? You cannot afford any surprises at this stage. If there is someone attending whom you are not familiar with, ask your key contact for an immediate briefing on the person's role. Why will the individual be there and what role will he or she have in the decision-making process? If at all possible, arrange for a conference call or a face-to-face visit. The customer may not be able to accommodate your request so late in the game, but you need to ask.

Allow for Customer Participation

When I discussed the sales discovery process in Chapter 5, I suggested that you ask a sixth question: "Is there anything else I need to know to make you as successful as possible in this sales process?" The reason for asking this question is to ensure the best possible sales discovery process. Now that you are in the finalist presentation, you want the exact same result.

A finalist presentation is like the World Series for sales professionals. You do not want to look back at your performance and feel as though you did not give it 100 percent. You want to give it your best shot. And one way you can give it that best shot is to provide for customer feedback during the presentation itself.

After reviewing the customer's needs and objectives, I always go to a flip chart and give the participants the opportunity to add needs or objectives. I do this, even this late in the sales process, because I want to make sure that I fully understand what they are trying to accomplish. (Please note that I have asked for the flip chart in advance of the presentation. This is not something that you want to leave to chance.)

Yes, acknowledging that I may have neglected some needs or objectives could be viewed as a flaw in the presentation. But I would much rather have this flaw exposed than to let some needs go unaddressed. And, on balance, giving the customer the opportunity to add points can help position you for success.

First, if the customer does not or cannot add anything else, that serves as an announcement that your sales discovery process was successful, which is not a trivial point. Second, if the customer does add a need or objective at this late stage, it gives you the opportunity to respond on the fly, accommodating the new need in your presentation. There is probably nothing worse than an unmet need or concern at this late stage. Yes, you may have missed something earlier, but at least you can address it now.

Present Your Solution

In the movie *Philadelphia*, Denzel Washington, as the attorney for an AIDS-stricken Tom Hanks, was often heard to say to a witness, "Please explain this to me as if I were a six-year-old." Like Denzel Washington in the courtroom, who did not intend any disrespect to the jurors, you do not mean any disrespect to the customer's purchasing committee when you describe your solution. The point, though, is that you need to be as clear as possible when presenting your solution.

Figure 9.2 shows how your solution is mapped to customer needs. There should be very little doubt in your mind, and in the minds of those on the purchasing committee, that your solution is very much on target at this point.

But while you have crafted an excellent solution, you have not demonstrated that your solution is the *best* solution for the customer at this point. All you have done is shown that your solution will meet their needs. To demonstrate that your solution is the best solution, you need to respond to any objections

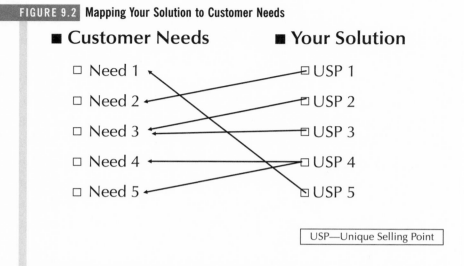

FIGURE 9.2 Mapping Your Solution to Customer Needs

or concerns. After addressing those concerns, you then demonstrate that you provide the best value for the investment and that your solution will work with either the highest degree of certainty or the lowest degree of risk.

Customer Objections During a Presentation

One of the points that I make in all of my books is based on the concept of "five unique selling points" or a company's five greatest strengths in the market. The reason I use the number 5 is that sales lore has it that most sales take place after the fifth call, yet most sales people quit after the first call. So, if most sales take place after the fifth call, I concluded that it would be good to always have five answers to the question, "Why should I do business with you?" This way, no matter where you are in the sales process, you can give the customer yet another reason to speak with you on the phone, yet another reason to meet with you face to face, and yet another reason to do business with you—all without sounding repetitive.

The unfortunate fact is that, while your company has its five unique selling points, so does the competition, whether they are aware of them or not. So, your job is to raise the visibility of your company's unique selling points. That is also the job of the competitive sales person, and you could easily argue that the sales person who does the best job of this will win the sale. This is especially true at this final stage of the sales process.

Visualize your task as a pair of scales. You have your strengths, and so does the competition. The customer uses the scale to weigh the value of your strengths against those of the competition. The company that brings the most value (strengths) to the customer will likely win the business.

Unfortunately, the process of winning or losing the sale is not as easy as tipping the scales. Remember that the competition has been championing their solutions and raising the visibility of their strengths as well. While you are presenting your solution, raising the visibility of your company's strengths, and generally championing your cause, the customer may well recall a strength of the competition. Instead of listening to your presentation, the customer is forming a question. First the hand goes up to get your attention, and then you stop speaking to acknowledge the question.

Without referring to the competition, the customer asks you about one of their strengths. Because he or she is asking you about a strength of the competition, it is not a strength of yours and you can be caught in a difficult position. However, this is only a difficult position if you are not prepared. (You must realize by now that preparation is one of my key messages in this book.) The good news is that, irrespective of how many competitors there are, there are only a handful of significant ones in any given market—the remainder are typically smaller, less consequential organizations. As a result, it is relatively easy to prepare for the objections you will hear during your presentation.

Preparation Is Key

If your sales discovery process was solid, you can rank your five unique selling points in the customer's order of preference. First, this allows you to focus on the one or two points that are really important to the customer and reinforce those points in the presentation—this is known as the "hot-button close."

Second, should you receive an unexpected time limitation to your presentation, you can easily cover the key points in order of preference to the customer. Not only do you rank your unique selling points in order of customer preference, you should also know what the competition's unique selling points are. With only one or two significant competitors to deal with, you prioritize their unique selling points in potential order of preference to the customer to get a good idea of the "damaging thoughts" that the competition has been whispering in the customer's ear.

When the customer raises his or her hand and asks you that one, humbling question, then you can respond with, "That's a great point and I agree with you on that. However, what you might find even more important is. . . ." Then you segue into one of your unique selling points, presumably the one at the top of the customer's priority list.

Objections, whether they occur early in the sales process, as discussed in Chapter 6, or during a finalist presentation, are typically few in number and repetitive. I am not going to suggest that you can prepare for 100 percent of potential objections. There will be times when you get caught unprepared, no matter how much preparation work you do.

However, there is an old saying, "Fool me once, shame on you. Fool me twice, shame on me." After hearing the same objection a few times in a row, you should be able to understand the challenge you face and prepare for that objection in the next transaction. The key to objection handling, whether in a finalist presentation or in a sales discovery meeting, is preparation. With proper preparation, over the long run the number of times that you will be caught off guard will be minimal.

Summarize Why the Customer Should Select You

Your presentation is drawing to a close, and it's time to summarize why the customer should select you. As you know, your list of unique selling points is tailor-made for this purpose, especially when ranked in the customer's order of importance. However, if you really want to do a great job on the presentation, take the time to elaborate on the potential financial impact of your solution on the customer's business.

When you start to wrap up your presentation, you need to understand one very important and sobering point: in all likelihood, your product or service will work just fine in the customer's application—but so will the competition's. There are only two ways to differentiate your solution in the eyes of the customer. One is your unique selling points and the other is the part of your solution that addresses the customer's niche needs.

Remember, a niche need is one that the customer cannot readily fill in the market. It is a need that is possibly hard to identify in the first place, and if identified, is hard to find a suitable provider. If you have followed the strategies for success presented throughout this book, you should be well positioned at this point. Both your unique selling points and the niche needs that you uncovered in your sales discovery process will help you differentiate your solution from that of the competition.

Acknowledge the Value Added

Most customers acknowledge the pleasure they get when value is added to a business solution, either through servicing niche needs or through other types of value added. What they are generally unwilling to do is acknowledge that your added value actually has a financial impact on their business.

Once a customer acknowledges that added value by recognizing its financial impact on the business, the sales process is usually over. So, if you can demonstrate that the customer receives a better return on the investment with you than they would with the competition, the game is over and you have won.

In the summary, you not only want to review the unique selling points, in order of customer preference, and the niche needs that are filled through your solution, but also call out the potential financial impact of those benefits. Keep in mind that any element of your solution the customer values has a financial impact on their business; otherwise, why would they value it?

To emphasize the financial impact of a value point in your solution, just ask the customer a few questions. Let me illustrate by way of a simple example. Whenever I shop for a new car, I always look for a dealership that services cars over the weekend. Why? Because this is something that is important to me, something that I value.

Let us assume that I have found the car of my dreams, and there are two dealerships in town that have that car. One dealership is located on the north side of town and the other dealership is on the south side. Both dealerships have the exact car I am looking for and both dealerships are offering the same price. Also, both dealerships are the same distance from my home. There is only one difference—the dealer on the north side of town allows me to have my car serviced on Saturdays, instead of missing valuable work time during the week.

Let us assume that my salary is $50 per hour, and that I would have to service my car, on average, four times a year. Let us also assume that I "acquired" the car on a three-year lease so the car would need servicing twelve times over the life of the lease. My final assumption is that it would take three hours to service the car each time. I would have to drive to the dealership, wait until my car is serviced, and then drive back to work. In total, I would be spending 36 hours (three hours per service times twelve services over the course of the lease) servicing my car during the lease. Since I make $50 per hour, the cost to me of selecting the car without the availability of Saturday service would be $1,800.

Let's take this example one step further, because it will be quite eye-opening to do so. We all know that it is customary to negotiate the purchase price of a car. Assuming that the price of the car is $30,000, a good negotiator would feel proud negotiating a $1,000 discount on such a car. It would not be uncommon for you and the sales person to go back and forth on the purchase price until you finally settled on a discounted price.

Most sales people are not astute enough to realize that the Saturday service option is worth $1,800 to a buyer, and that they should be able to minimize their discounting, simply by pointing out the value added to the base price of the car. So, quantifying the impact of your solution on the customer's business can have a significant impact, and as you summarize the reasons the customer should do business with you, be sure to point out that advantage.

The Value in the Sales Relationship

The value-management question that you asked during the sales discovery process is particularly relevant to the finalist presentation: "What do you value in a relationship with a company like ours?" You can use the customer's response to this question to convey the value that the customer will realize if your solution is chosen.

Returning to the car dealership example, we can assume that a normal car sales person might ask the buyer questions about color preference, desired engine size, and importance of sound systems. A great sales person would ask those same questions, but would ask them in another way, such as "What do you value in a relationship with a car dealership such as ours?" or "What are the types of things that you are looking for in the car itself?"

Remember the difference between open-ended questions and closed-ended questions, discussed in Chapter 5? Closed-ended questions such as, "Do you prefer the black car or the gray car?" "Do you prefer the larger engine or the smaller engine?" or "Do you prefer the standard sound system or the upgraded sound system?" give you buyer information—there is no disputing that. However, because these questions are closed-ended, and because you ask them too early in the sales cycle, you are not gathering all of the information you require to be successful. You only get the information that you request.

A quality open-ended question, such as "What do you value in a relationship with a car dealership such as ours?" gets the buyer to reveal crucial information that can help you in this transaction. A question like this would reveal my need to have car service available on the weekends. Once the sales person understands that I need service over the weekend, their next question could be as simple as "Why?" This would prompt me to tell the sales person about the cost of missing work.

A great salesperson would then ask follow-up questions until he or she had gathered the information required to calculate the value to me of the dealer's solution. A sample discussion along these lines is as follows:

SALES PERSON: What do you value in a relationship with a car dealership like ours?

CUSTOMER: I need a dealership that is open on the weekend for servicing.

SALES PERSON: Why is that important to you?

CUSTOMER: Because I will miss work.

SALES PERSON: Why are you so concerned about missing work?

CUSTOMER: Because I only get paid on an hourly basis when I work.

SALES PERSON: Well, how many times do you believe a car will need service during the year?

CUSTOMER: Four.

SALES PERSON: And how many years will you be leasing your car for?

CUSTOMER: Three.

SALES PERSON: I had a friend who used to work in a position similar to yours. He used to make about $50 per hour. Is that about correct?

CUSTOMER: Yes.

SALES PERSON: Do you realize what we just did?

CUSTOMER: No, not really.

SALES PERSON: You said that a car requires service *on average four times* per year, and I know that it takes *three hours per service call* to service the car. That amounts to *twelve hours of service* each year. You said that you will lease the car for three years, which means that the total service time requirement over the life of the car is thirty-six service calls. If you assume the $50 per hour of salary we used earlier, the *value* of the weekend service to you is $1,800.

CUSTOMER: Hmmmm. I guess that you are right.

SALES PERSON: Yes, and you were looking to buy the car at a $900 discount, correct?

CUSTOMER: Yes, that's correct.

SALES PERSON: Well, I can offer you $450 of that discount in cash and I can offer you an additional $1,800 in savings related to the availability of weekend service. How does that sound? Do we have a deal?

CUSTOMER: Yes, we do. Thank you for being so helpful.

By the end of this conversation, the sales person has called out the hidden value built into the solution.

One Important Word of Caution

Calculating the value built into a solution may seem like a bit of magic, but it is really just an extension of the sales discovery process developed in Chapter 5. All it requires is that you become a bit more astute in listening to the information that the customer is providing. Of course this type of calculation is not something you can spring on the meeting participants at the end of the sales cycle. It must be integrated into your sales process, but you can use the presentation summary to remind the listeners of this additional value built into your business solution.

Provide a Compelling Reason to Act

This is a relatively easy portion of the presentation, coming on the heels of your summary. Figure 9.1 listed the seven points of an effective sales presentation. Points 1 and 2 are when you make 100 percent certain that you understand the customer's needs. Point 3 is when you tell the customer that you have a solution that meets those stated needs. Point 4 is when you minimize any strengths that the competitive solution may have over your solution, and point 5 is when you reinforce the strengths of your solution in relation to the competition, largely through your summary.

At this point in the presentation, you have positioned yourself as the unique, best solution to the customer's needs. Now your only competitor is *inaction*—and that is perhaps your greatest competitor of all. But let's look at an example of this and see how the situation can be turned around.

In 1995 I was working on a major request for proposal just about the time that I sold my first company. Because of the size of this proposal, the customer's major decision-making point was to select the company that could complete the solution the fastest, yet at the same time maintain a quality level sufficient to ensure success of the project. The project was an extremely large computer-training application, and the customer wanted to get up and running as fast as possible.

To make a long story short, we were awarded the business. In fact, the customer made its decision about one month prior to my departure from the company I had founded. We were awarded the contract on the basis of the belief that we could complete the training in the shortest time possible and still maintain quality. The funny part was that, during the entire month prior to my departure, the contract never got implemented—in spite of the fact that the decision was based on time needs.

When I called to say hello to a couple of former co-workers about a month later, I heard that the contract was in the same situation—awarded but not implemented. Then I called back one quarter, one half-year, and one year later and found that the contract status had still not changed!

This situation gives me a good opportunity to demonstrate how to handle a frustrating situation. You are waiting for a decision to be made. You call the customer week after week, month after month, asking if a supplier has been selected, if the customer is ready to get started. That approach can be quite annoying after the first few calls.

The Opportunity Costs of Slow Decision Making

Opportunity costs are not "real" costs, in the sense that you are paying bills. Rather, they are the cost—or lost income—of *not* doing something. In the case of your presentation, the customer experiences opportunity costs by not making the purchase and implementing the solution. Time lost in correcting a problem *does* cost a business money. That's why it is in the best interests of the customer to act—to select a supplier and get going.

Although my example from the computer-training business involved a contract awarded, the situation is the same because the solution wasn't implemented. Let us assume that the customer was looking to improve workforce productivity by 5 percent as a result of the computer training we were to implement. What I would do is show the customer the opportunity cost of *not* implementing our solution. For the sake of simplicity, assume that there were 100 people designated to receive the training. (The calculation of the cost is not a function of the magnitude of your solution. Larger solutions will, of course, re-sult in larger opportunity costs, but the calculation itself is not a function of the magnitude of the solution.)

We can also assume that the average salary of these individu-als is $50,000 per year, and that the customer assigns a factor of 200 percent relating to benefits and overhead. A benefits and overhead factor accounts for the fact that the cost of maintaining someone on the company payroll is usually more than the cost of that person's direct salary alone. These costs include the man-agement infrastructure to support the employees, employees' va-cation time, training expenses, medical benefits, and such. Benefits and overheads can range from a low of 120 percent at the smallest of companies in the United States to as high as 280 percent in large, global corporations. Customers know their benefits and overhead factor.

Doing the Numbers

Figure 9.3 shows how to calculate the opportunity cost—in this case, of not implementing the contracted solution. As you can see, the opportunity cost here is approximately $42,000 per month. This is the amount of money the customer forgoes sav-ing (or earning) every month that a decision is delayed. It's not a small loss.

I suggest that you use this as a compelling reason to get your customer to act—to decide on a supplier. Show the intended savings or proposed increased earnings that your solution will bring and contrast that figure with the opportunity cost of not proceeding with your solution. Remember, also, that all of the suggestions for earlier calculations with regard to added value apply here as well.

Any time you prepare financial calculations as part of your

FIGURE 9.3 **Opportunity Cost Calculation**

Number of people in department	100
Average salary	$50,000
Benefits and overhead factor	200%
Total fully loaded labor cost	$10,000,000
Productivity enhancement	$500,000
Monthly productivity enhancement	~$42,000

sales effort, you must have extensive customer input and support in deriving your bottom line. Otherwise, you will have a difficult time having those calculations accepted at the time of your presentation.

Remember Your Follow-Through

If you are the first presenter at the finals, there is going to be a time lag between when you make your presentation and when the customer makes the decision. If you do nothing during that time, including the time when the competition makes their presentations, my strategy of going first and being the standard bearer can possibly work against you.

The benefit to going first is, as mentioned earlier in this chapter, to set the bar high—to command the playing field. The major risk in this strategy is that the competitions' more recent presentations may seem clearer in the customer's mind. That's why it is so important that you do *not* become a distant memory.

You need to let the customer know that you are still watching out for his or her best interests, even after you have made your presentation.

One easy way to show this interest is to use Google Alerts, a tool I mentioned earlier in this book. Google Alerts will help you stay abreast of the news as it relates to your customer and his or her industry. Make certain you have a Google Alert set up for the company. When you see a newsworthy item, convert it into an e-mail attachment and send it along with a thought-provoking cover e-mail. This tells the customer that you care about the decision, that you care about their business, and that you are not sitting by idly, waiting. Rather, you are continuing to differentiate your solution from those of the competition and continuing to add value to the customer's business.

The Google Alerts tactic represents another way you can manage customer perceptions—of you, your solution, and your company. By extending the sales process beyond the presentation you also increase your chances of being selected. The customer recognizes your interest in the business and acknowledges the value you continue to add—thereby acknowledging what's important in a relationship with your company.

I don't know how many deals this technique has won me, because I have never been privy to customers' thoughts about our proposals at the time they received a newsworthy article from me. However, I suspect that this has been a big asset over the years. When I started using this approach, it was more difficult to implement because everything had to be done manually, using regular postal mail. Now, with the Internet, e-mail, and Google Alerts, the process takes minimal effort.

*   *   *

So here we are, at the end of Part III of the book and at the end of the sales process. This Red Hot Sales Process—Plan, Execute, Close—has shown itself to be an effective tool for increasing your chances of sales success.

If nothing else, I hope you have gotten two things out of this book. First, sales is a fully integrated process in which the activities of one phase enhance your chances of success in other phases. That is, what you do in the planning and execution phases has a clear and direct impact on your ability to close the sale and win the business. Second, that sales is a science, not an art. The field of sales is not for those who have the "gift of gab"; it is not for those who are unable to put the customer's best interests at the top of their priorities.

Sales is a *process* that can be dissected, analyzed, and improved upon. Listening, not talking, is one of your most important skills. The key to selling success is building long-term customer relationships, and to do that you must always place the customer's interests above your own. Sales people derive their success from the success of their customers, not in spite of their customer's success.

In the final chapter, I share with you a few thoughts on what I consider to be the Ten Best Sales Strategies.

CHAPTER 10

The Ten Best Sales Strategies

I have been a sales professional for twenty-six years. In concluding this book, I want to provide you with the Ten Best Sales Strategies that I have developed during this time. These are powerful ideas, techniques, and strategies that have taken me an entire career to learn and develop. In one way or another, they have all been discussed in this book. However, by summarizing them here, you can jump-start your Red Hot Selling sales career. These ten ideas are my guiding light for the remainder of my days in the field. I hope that they will be yours as well.

Strategy 1: Sales Is a Process

Always remember that sales is a process—and a process can always be improved. Our sales process is: Plan, Execute, Close.

If you are not performing up to your expectations, or up to the expectations of your company, you needn't wonder why. You are not on a streak of bad luck and you are not receiving the "bad" leads, which were talked about so prominently in the movie *Glengarry Glen Ross* as the reason for poor sales performance.

What you need to do is determine which step in your sales process is responsible for your suboptimal performance, and then improve that one element. Once you have done that, you can measure your performance improvement and determine if additional changes need to be made to further improve your performance. If necessary, isolate the weakest link in the sales process and make the requisite improvement. Continue this until your level of performance rises to your or your company's expectations.

One of the companies I worked with had an unusually low ratio of meetings to opportunities. This was easy to see, based on weekly prospecting reports. It's usually the result of not asking good, open-ended consultative selling questions at the start of the sales discovery process. An excellent way to fix this situation is with the Meeting Management Worksheet (see Chapter 5). Once instituted, sales personnel experienced a $1 million improvement in their sales pipeline for each percentage point improvement in their ratio of meetings to opportunities.

We now know that great sales people are made by selecting a successful sales process, and then following that process as closely as possible. Like a good recipe for a particular culinary delight, once you start changing the ingredients, the results start to disappoint. Remember, sales is a process: Plan, Execute, Close.

Strategy 2: Sales Time Management

Time management in the area of sales is divided into three broad categories. The first is nonselling activities, and the remaining two categories are prospecting activities and opportunity-management activities.

Because the sales person has little, if any, control over the amount of time he or she spends on nonselling activities, and because nonselling activities tend not to vary in magnitude across different sales levels, we can remove these activities from a seller's time-management equation. This means that sales time management comes down to one question: "How do I divide my time between opportunity management and prospecting?"

Sales people worldwide tend to overinvest in opportunity management, to the detriment of prospecting or opportunity identification. To control for this overinvestment in opportunity management, you need to make a fixed and measurable commitment to prospecting based on the number of dials per day or per week that you are going to make. The need to prospect is typically determined by the size of your current sales pipeline. It can also be impacted by where you are in a given quarter or year. However, the primary driving factor is the adequacy of your sales pipeline. You need to re-evaluate this commitment at the end of each month, as the need to prospect or the need to manage existing opportunities constantly changes.

Strategy 3: A Full Sales Pipeline

I have said this, in one way or another, in each of my four books: A full sales pipeline is the best sales strategy in the world, bar none!

There are so many options that a full pipeline gives you. For example, it allows you to properly represent your company in a sales negotiation. It gives you the courage to prepare a proper, value-based proposal and stick to your proposal even when the customer asks for a steep discount. It allows you to make proper sales decisions throughout the year, even at quarter ends and year ends.

There is no part of the sales process that is *not* impacted by a full, or not full, sales pipeline. And the only way to ensure that you have a full sales pipeline is to make a fixed and measurable commitment to the prospecting process. Not only do you need to commit to new-business development but you also need to assess the adequacy of that commitment. If your commitment is to make only two dials per day or ten dials per week, there is a chance that this is not sufficient to achieve your objectives. You may need to do more!

One of my clients this year was making two dials per day at the start of the year. At the half-year point, on June 30, he decided to increase the number of dials to four a day because the original commitment was not sufficient to meet the sales goals. That meant that the number of dials made for the second half of the year increased by 100 percent, the number of opportunities increased by 89 percent, and the value of the opportunities identified increased by 146 percent. In sales, there is a simple rule: If you do nothing, you get nothing; if you want more, you have to do more.

Strategy 4: The Large-Account Strategy

The secret of top performance is out: have a large-account strategy. When I say "large" that does not mean that you need to pursue every company in the world the size of GE or IBM. Rather, define *large* as large in your given target market. Even if you are targeting the mid-market or the small and medium business market (SMB), you can still have large accounts. A large account is an account from which you derive a significant and continuing revenue stream.

There are three categories of sales professionals, based on performance—new, moderate, and top. A new sales person produces very little in the way of current revenue. A moderate sales person brings in a middle level of revenue. A top performer needs no introduction—it is the professional who is "best in class" for the industry. The difference between new and moderate sellers is a few large accounts. The difference between moderate and top sellers is a few more large accounts. This means that the difference between new and top sellers is *a lot* of large accounts.

Large accounts typically come from large prospects, though this does not mean that large accounts cannot come from the smaller companies in your market. However, large prospects have a much better chance of becoming large accounts. If your goal is to become a top performer, you must focus on how to obtain your first large account. Once obtained, you then focus on obtaining your second large account, and so on.

A large account gives you both a significant and continuing revenue stream, and you begin to build your "base." Your base is the amount of revenue that you start with each month or each quarter without having to make additional sales. Your base comes from prior sales to your large accounts. Because you can earn revenue today from sales made in the past, you focus on finding your next large account and building your base even higher. This is the large-account strategy, and it's the way to become a top performer in your business.

Strategy 4a: The Corollary to the Large-Account Strategy

In some industries, such as the mortgage industry or others that focus on individual consumers, there is a corollary to the large-account strategy: Find the largest potential client level to work with before implementing the large-account strategy.

For example, in the mortgage industry, you might think that

it is best to work with individual homeowners because they are the ones who require the mortgages. However, mortgage companies changed their target market to focus on realtors. Why? Because one realtor could refer a sales person to many individuals requiring mortgages. Since it takes a similar amount of time to sell the realtor on your credibility as it does to sell to an individual, it is more time-efficient to focus on the realtor.

What the mortgage companies didn't realize, however, was that realtors were not the largest potential customer level they could work with. They could sell to an entire real estate office, getting all of the agents in the office to work with them at the same time. Thus, the large-account strategy is applied to a broader level, impacting sales growth and sales productivity dramatically.

Likewise, a client that sells SAT preparation courses to college-bound high school students grew their business exponentially by using the corollary. Previously they were selling to high schools, not individual high school students. When they started selling to school districts instead, sales growth and productivity accelerated. Therefore, the corollary to the large-account strategy is to apply it to the highest possible level within your target market.

Strategy 5: The Account Development Cycle

Building sales and account relationships is a step-by-step, incremental process called the "account development cycle." This cycle is the most efficient to build a lasting, fruitful sales relationship.

All too often, sales people start with a prospect and expect to win the grand prize—a large deal, a national account, or a global account. It would be wonderful if that is how sales works. I am not going to say that it never works that way, but when it does, I prefer to attribute the result to luck rather than a well-developed sales strategy. Building an account relationship takes place one step at a time. The account development cycle moves you from step to step, finding unique ways to serve the customer, or niche needs, and differentiating between winning a sale and growing an account relationship.

Often, companies, especially public companies, place too much emphasis on reaching quarterly sales goals, to the exclusion and detriment of long-term revenue sources. There is nothing in the account development cycle that is inconsistent with reaching sales goals. It simply is an effective model with which you can grow your account relationships. It helps you set proper sales goals at the account level that lead to both achievement of sales goals and growing market share.

Very simply, you start with the largest account in your market (using the large-account strategy) and grow your market share from zero to 100 percent. (I realize that it is not possible to have 100 percent market share at most accounts, but let's assume that it is possible for purposes of this discussion.) Now, you move to the second largest account in the market and repeat the process—grow your market share from zero to 100 percent.

If you follow this process at the third largest account, then go on to the fourth, fifth, sixth, and smaller accounts on the list, your market share is growing and the market share of the competition is getting smaller. The interesting point is that it is easier to make additional sales at the same account than it is to find new accounts. Therefore, following the account development cycle and using a relationship-based approach will grow your revenue much faster than will a transactional approach to sales. Over time, you will assume a dominant position in the market and your competition will be minimized. The account development cycle and relationship-based sales provide a superior approach.

Strategy 6: Planning: The Best Closing Strategy

This is probably the least intuitive of the ten strategies I present. Sales planning is the bane of the sales profession, yet it is the best closing strategy. There are leverage points to be worked in the sales process, and these are especially evident at closing.

Archimedes, the great Greek mathematician, said, "Give me a place to stand and with a lever I will move the whole world." While I cannot claim that a good sales planning tool will move the world, I can tell you that a good sales planning tool can dramatically impact your sales performance. Chapter 7 discussed closing techniques and showed that sales planning can give you the leverage to have a material impact on your sales results.

If you consider your incremental sales derived through sound sales planning and the commissions you receive on those incremental sales, you will realize that the time invested in planning is not wasted. Rather, it gives you an excellent return on your investment.

When you talk to sales people from every corner of the world, you will always hear that planning takes too much time away from "selling." While I am sure that some sales reports are excessive and possibly even unnecessary, that does not excuse you from considering the value of sales planning. I have often said that a sales person's commodity of purchase is time. By "commodity of purchase," I draw a comparison between time in the sales world and money in the nonsales world. That is, when you want to buy something in the nonsales world, you do so with money.

For most of us, money is a limited commodity and so we choose how we spend and invest our money. If we spend all of our money frivolously and invest nothing, we will probably have a great time now, but our future prospects will be limited. In the sales profession, time bears many of the same traits as money in the real world. If we spend our time frivolously, we will have a great time now but our sales future will be limited.

All of us, no matter who we are, have a limited amount of time. There are only 24 hours in the day, and we can only work some lesser amount of that. It stands to reason that a sales person must be smart about how he or she invests time. In fact, the limited allocation of time, along with the need to invest it wisely, is the single driving factor underlying the large-account strategy. Because we have a limited amount of time, we must sell as much as we can in the time that we have available. The large-account strategy does this for you, providing the accounts that are most likely to result in large and recurring revenues.

Sales planning provides no immediate pleasure, but it is like money in the bank when it comes to closing the deal. When objections arise, when questions are asked, the planning you have done will provide the ready answers.

Strategy 7: Monitoring Your Progress

Monitoring your progress is a powerful sales strategy. There are many reasons to monitor, but here are two major ones.

First, sales reports create accountability. Accountability drives superior performance. That is why we must measure our progress. My favorite example of the power of accountability comes from my first experience at Weight Watchers, the popular weight-loss program. When you start, you get an introductory lecture that explains how the program works. One element of the introductory program is the "weekly meal report," which has sections for each day of the week and subsections for the meals that you eat during a day. For each day of the week, there is a section for breakfast, lunch, and dinner, as well as two snacks, one in the mid-morning and one in the mid-afternoon.

The instructor holds up the report, looks everyone straight in the eye, and says, "If you write down everything that you eat in this report, you will lose weight." She also says, "If you don't write down everything that you eat in this booklet, you will not lose weight." The idea behind this is that it takes time to write everything down, and once you do, you realize how much you have eaten. This is standard diet regimen. More philosophically, however, members are held accountable for what they do and don't do. There is no way to hide from the truth. If you don't record what you eat, your performance suffers.

The same is true in sales. If you compare your results to your plans, you are holding yourself accountable for your results. And when you can see where results have not met expectations, you can improve.

I have a friend who is an executive sales manager at a global technology and services company. We have a program that we implement at clients that always generates a significant sales result improvement, and I approached him about it. At first he was resistant. Yet over the years he became its single most successful proponent. When I asked him why he felt the program worked, he responded in one word: "Accountability!"

The second key point about monitoring is that sales is a forgiving profession. A sales year, your primary accountability period, is divided into four quarters, twelve months, and fifty-two weeks. Each of these smaller periods is associated with one of the three sales planning tools. Proper use of these tools, along with monitoring your progress, gives you the opportunity to make many adjustments along the way. None of us has a crystal ball to predict the future. Estimates are just that—estimates. The plan may or may not be on target. This does not make you a good sales person or a bad sales person. It simply means that some of your assumptions require adjustment, but you will know that only if you monitor your progress.

Strategy 8: Managing Customer Perceptions

You have 365 days a year to work with your customers and help them understand the proper decision-making criteria for the purchase of your products or services. If you wait to the point of sale to have input you will be doomed to compete on price.

Since you cannot change your company's value propositions in the short term, and you cannot change the value propositions of your competitors in the market, your only option in the sales process is to manage customer perceptions. That is, you need to make your customers think through the proposals. And not only do you want your customers to think, you need them to think properly. That is, they need to view your value additions above those of the competition.

Managing customer perceptions leads to a sustainable sales and business strategy. In sales, you want to be the person who goes first, who sets the bar, who determines the standards. You do this by presenting a comprehensive solution that fills not only the customer's core needs but also the niche needs—those not readily apparent to the competition.

You accomplish this by managing the customer's decision-making. To the extent that you are successful in managing your customer's decision-making process, the result of doing so will be reflected in your sales results. In fact, you reach the ultimate in sales and the pinnacle of success when you help the customer develop their decision-making criteria.

Strategy 9: Being Prepared

An Olympic athlete prepares for a lifetime in order to achieve that one moment in the spotlight. Sprinters, for instance, enter an event that lasts less than 10 seconds, yet they prepare for many years. Why? Because they want to win. And so do sales people!

You need to prepare for your sales events—the initial prospecting call, the face-to-face sales discovery meeting, and the sales negotiation. You need to prepare for these events just as if you were preparing for the 100-yard dash.

This book is all about preparation. Each chapter detailed the steps to take and the results you could expect. Now that you have the luxury to look back on the sales process I have described and reflect on what has been recommended, I think you will agree that, in any given area, the preparation required is not overbearing. Compared to that of the Olympic athlete, sales people have the better deal.

The deal even gets better when you leverage your preparation over a long career. The same cannot be said for the Olympic athlete, whose body quickly wears out. In our case, if you adapt good habits early on in your sales career, you can reap the rewards for many years to come, possibly for the duration of a forty-year career.

Strategy 10: The Roadmap to Success

I thought it only appropriate that the last strategy be a tribute to my mother—a sales giant in her own right.

When I first started in my sales career, I purchased an audio-cassette program by Brian Tracy, a renowned sales trainer in his day. As I listened to his program, there were several things that stood out in my mind. One was, "God gave us two ears and one mouth and we (professional sales people) should use them in that proportion."

While I don't agree that the proportion of listening to speaking has to be a fixed ratio, I do believe that this is an excellent starting point for a sales career. This is, in essence, my mother's recommendation as well when she said, "The customer will always show you the roadmap to success." Listening to your customer is paramount for sales success.

Consultative selling and value selling are collaborative processes involving you and your customer, as well as your company and the customer's company. You cannot be a consultative "solution seller" without the participation of your customer. You cannot add value to his or her business without that individual's help. Too often, sales people sit in their offices and believe that they know what is right for the customers. This belief couldn't be further from the truth.

A short time ago, I attended a meeting on behalf of one of my customers. The goal was to accelerate sales growth, but the company had traditionally relied on word of mouth and after trying several different sales approaches on their own, concluded that they didn't work. This is where I entered the equation. I asked few questions on behalf of the company I was working for. By the end of the meeting, I concluded that my client did not know its customer very well.

My client had never taken the time to visit the customer and had never toured the facility. If he had, he would have found the situation different from what he assumed. My client, on the other hand, was safely nestled away in his office, applauding himself for a job well done.

That client was a young and growing company, but it had much to learn if the bright future it envisioned would be realized. You see, you can't have a roadmap to success unless you take the time to understand your customers, and that involves listening.

In contrast, another of my clients is in the solar energy field. I went with that client on a sales call to a new account. The new account was interested in the green technology and showed off the building where they intended to place the panels. The problem was that the building was old and inappropriate for a long-term investment such as solar panels. That building would never last as long as the panels would, and the investment in solar energy would go down with the building. However, since we were on the customer site, we were able to see all of their buildings and recommend other, more appropriate locations. This was an excellent example of filling a niche need for the customer, achieved by listening and observing, and it assured that the client had a roadmap to success.

*   *   *

I started this book by asking if you want to be a sales professional. I hope that I have helped you answer that question. Sales is a great profession with unlimited income potential, the ability to be highly creative, and the opportunity to learn and grow with your industry as the world evolves. I wish you the best in your sales career and hope that your remaining years in our profession will be RED HOT!

Index